*Why in the world should*
GINGER ROGERS and LUCILLE BALL
*wash dishes for*
HENRY FONDA and JIMMY STEWART?

What's it like to have BARBARA STANWYCK
become your houseguest? Or to interview knife-
toting members of THE MANSON FAMILY?
Or to watch MAE WEST order the president of
her fan club to "Dance for the little lady, dance!"
when *you're* the little lady?

SHIRLEY EDER

*tells it all in*

*NOT THIS TIME, CARY GRANT!*

# Not This Time, Cary Grant!

**************************************
And Other Stories About Hollywood
**************************************

## Shirley Eder

BANTAM BOOKS · TORONTO · NEW YORK · LONDON

NOT THIS TIME, CARY GRANT!
*A Bantam Book / published by arrangement with
Doubleday & Company, Inc.*

*PRINTING HISTORY*
*Doubleday edition published October 1973*
*2nd printing ..... October 1973*
*Bantam edition published November 1974*

*Bantam Books are published by Bantam Books, Inc. Its trade-
mark, consisting of the words "Bantam Books" and the portrayal of a bantam, is registered in the United States Patent
Office and in other countries. Marca Registrada. Bantam
Books, Inc., 666 Fifth Avenue, New York, New York 10019.*

PRINTED IN THE UNITED STATES OF AMERICA

*For my father, who still believes this is something I'm going to grow out of.*

*And for my husband, Edward, who so patiently helped me to grow.*

# Contents

# The True Test of Friendship

Have you ever thought about which of your close pals would show up at your funeral?

One summer Sunday afternoon, my husband, Edward, and I were sitting around talking about important things like that. You see, it was raining and he couldn't play golf, so he stayed home and talked with me. It isn't every husband who stays home to talk with his wife after twenty-odd years of marriage, so I was grateful for any discussion—even funerals.

So many of my friends are in show business, and show folk are notoriously preoccupied with their own affairs. Edward asked, "Do you think Missy (Barbara Stanwyck) would come all the way from California for your funeral? Or Kathryn Grayson? or etc., etc.??"

Well, there was one way to tell—put it to the test. Systematically, I decided to call those closest to me. My husband said, "Don't bother with Ginger Rogers. She's a Christian Scientist, and they don't believe in death. When you go, to Ginger, you'll still be here, so that would be a wasted call."

"Kathryn Grayson will probably be the only one who'll come from anywhere for your funeral," continued Edward. "She'd walk out on a performance, if need be." That decided it—Katie was the first to test. I placed the call to her home in Santa Monica and was told that she was in rehearsal for *Rosalinda* at the Kenley Playhouse in Warren, Ohio.

The operator got the theatre and asked for Miss Kathryn Grayson.

"She's rehearsing outside and can't come to the phone," the voice on the other end said.

"Tell her it's *almost* an emergency," I prompted.

The voice said, "In that case, please wait."

After what seemed forever, on came the familiar voice, breathless: "Shirley—what's the matter?"

"Katie, when I die—will you come to my funeral?"

"Are you ill [worried]?"

I explained that I was perfectly well, and didn't expect to pass on to wherever it is one passes on to for a long while. I just wanted to know—that was all.

"You mean," she shouted, "you got me out of a rehearsal and made me run all this way, just to ask a hypothetical question? I don't think I'll ever forgive you for this."

As long as she was there, I insisted on an answer. There was a moment of thoughtful silence. Then she said: "Yes, I'll come, but I won't sing," and slammed the phone down.

Edward was right—I could count on Kathryn Grayson to come to my funeral, even if she never spoke to me again in my lifetime.

The next call was to Barbara Stanwyck in Beverly Hills, California.

We had a short discussion of the weather in Los Angeles, then wham—right to the point.

"Missy, when I die—will you come to my funeral?"

"Where will it be?"

"In Detroit, probably."

"Shirley," she said, "of course I'll come, *if* I'm not working. However, if I'm in the middle of the shooting of a movie or a television show, you know I won't be

2

there. I couldn't let the rest of the company down. Can't you have it in Los Angeles around lunchtime? Then I wouldn't have to take more than an hour off from work."

At the end of that call, I looked across the room at my husband, who, so far, had predicted two out of two. He was smiling the smile of an all-knowing SOB.

"Just one more long-distance call," he said. "We need to save some money for your funeral."

So I put in a call to Mitzi Gaynor, who also lives in Beverly Hills.

"Hello, Shirley—how are you?"

"Fine, Mitzi—how's Jack?"

"He's well, thank you. How's the weather back where I used to live?"

"It's lovely here today. Mitz—got something to ask you. When I die, would you fly here for my funeral?"

Dead silence—then: "Who else is gonna be there, Shirl?"

Mission accomplished. Two maybes, and one commitment. At least there would be one "name" at my funeral.

Edward, knowing I was a little disappointed, put his arms around me and said, "Don't worry, honey. I'll give you the kind of send-off you'll love. They put Abe Lincoln on a train and stopped at various depots along the way for the people to properly mourn. Honey—I'll put you on a plane, and we'll go to the Coast first, so all your movie pals can pay homage. Then I'll fly you back to Detroit for our civilian friends to view the body. Then, it's on to New York for your legitimate show-biz buddies—and then to Brooklyn for the burial."

*Brooklyn!* I never could find my way around there alive. No Brooklyn for me!

"Okay, honey," continued Edward, "I'll try to talk Vincent Sardi into letting me place you in a permanent crypt under booth number one. Then you can hear everything that's going on and can write a column called 'Eternally Yours.'"

That made me happy. I thanked him profusely until the thought came to me: "How come we're planning *my* funeral and not his?"

# A Whiff of Show Biz

After graduation from Friends Seminary in New York, I was supposed to go on to Bennington College, but the only thing I wanted to do was to go on the stage! I went to my father, a New York State Supreme Court Justice, who was still under the assumption that "life upon the wicked stage was nothing for a girl," (lyrics from *Show Boat*) and begged him to let me seek instead a career in show business. He relented to this extent: "It is now June. If you can get a job in a show before school starts in September, you don't have to go to college." That's how sure he was of my "untalent."

By golly, in August I got a job. It was in the last week of the last road company of *The Women*, which was to play for one week only, at the Adams Theatre in Newark, New Jersey.

I was given ten lines as the first girl in the fitting-room scene. During rehearsals I lost seven of the ten lines to an actress with whom the director was said to be having an affair. "Having an affair" sounds pretty corny now, but at the time I was plenty shocked!

During rehearsals I had become very friendly with a young actress named Celeste Holm. Celeste had been playing, all around the United States, the important role of Crystal, the girl in the-then shocking bathtub scene. Actually, you couldn't see any of Celeste's body because it was all covered up with bubbles, under which she wore a body stocking. But you should have heard the gasps in the audience at every performance.

I didn't know anything about makeup or anything else pertaining to the professional theatre. Celeste, feeling sorry for me, taught me a few of the necessaries. Somehow, having played the lead role in Jo in *Little Women* at Friends Seminary didn't qualify me even for the week in Newark (which isn't exactly Broadway).

I'd seen so many movies with themes of backstage stories, that I knew actresses received lots of opening-night telegrams. Sooooo, I sent myself one from the-then New York Governor Herbert Lehman, from the mayor of the city and from a couple of movie stars (who I never thought I'd meet later on in life, but did). Even now, when I'm with them I sometimes have small pangs of guilt. But my lips are sealed!

I shudder with embarrassment when I think how ridiculous I must have appeared to the real actresses in the dressing room. Those telegrams were pasted all over the mirror, which I shared with three girls. How they managed to get their eyelashes on straight through Joan Crawford's wire (oops—that's a confession), I'll never know.

My parents came from New York for the opening night. Somewhere in the middle of the play my father nudged my mother and asked, "When does Shirley come on?" My mother said, "Didn't you see her? She's already been on." When the final curtain came down, I met my parents who were waiting outside in a car because they were too ashamed to come backstage. Celeste Holm was with me. She lived only a block away from us on lower Fifth Avenue. Celeste and I sat in the back seat—my parents up front. I can hear my father now as he said in a determined voice: "You are going to college in September."

"But you promised," I whined. "If I got a job in the theatre before September I wouldn't have to go to college."

"That is true," said the Honorable Justice, "but I meant it only if you became a 'star' before September."

I can also recall, on that ride back from Newark, a really humiliating experience. Here I was, sitting next to a professional actress and heard my father lumping her with me—the rankest (rank in every sense of the word) amateur—by saying, "You girls ought to give up this business. The theatre is no place for you. Besides, you aren't going to get any place." Would you believe he was saying this to Celeste Holm?

About a year later, my parents went to see *Oklahoma!* on Broadway. My father nudged my mother and said, "How come that marvelous actress who just stopped the show singing 'I Can't Say No' looks familiar to me?"

"She should," said my ever-patient mother. "She was the girl who sat in the back seat of the car with your daughter, and you told them both they were never going to make it. Her name is Celeste Holm."

To this day, Celeste, a very close friend still, often says, "I should have listened to your father. The theatre is really no place for anyone!" That's when she's between jobs. When she is starring in a film, or in a play or on TV, you can bet Judge Eder's words never enter her mind. Celeste Holm will go down in the annals of show business as one of its most gifted actresses—despite the advice of Justice Morris Eder.

About Shirley Eder—he was absolutely right!

7

# Big-name Guests on Small-time Show

When I was seventeen years old, I had my first
radio show—a woman's show on station WINS in
New York. It was during the Second World War, so
on the show I read recipes sent to me from the OWI
and OPA in Washington. In other words, I would read
their pamphlets on how to prepare food with ersatz
ingredients. This wasn't exactly what I had in mind,
career-wise, but it did get me on radio at the same
time I was going to classes at New York University.

I wanted to interview show-business personalities,
not read silly recipes. Somehow, I managed to get
Broadway stars and movie personalities visiting New
York on public appearance tours to come on the air
and read the recipes along with me. Little by little
we did fewer and fewer recipes and talked more and
more about show business. The station was so delighted to get show-biz names for free, they accepted
my change of format without saying a word.

Arlene Francis was appearing on Broadway at the
time in a hit play called *The Doughgirls*. Up until the
day she guested on the show, I had always prepared
a written script. Arlene changed my entire style of
interviewing when she said, "Just let's talk."

8

I tore up the script and from that day to this I have ad-libbed any and every show I do on radio, TV and even on the lecture circuit.

There weren't that many interview programs on the air then, and press agents, I learned quickly, needed a place to plug their wares and the wares Broadway press agents sold were the shows and the actors in them. Word got around about our program, and good things began to happen.

Getting five or more guests a week to promise to come on was not a great chore, but getting them all to actually show up was. It was a morning show, and actors liked to stay up most of the night and sleep most of the day. When I started on WINS, the only star I could really call "friend" was Mitzi Green, who at the time was starring in the musical *Babes in Arms*. From the time Mitzi had been a kid star in pictures she was well known for her impersonations of other prominent stars.

When I say "friend" I mean friend in every sense of the word. My program went on the air at 11 A.M. Often earlier that same morning, a press agent would call to report that his star had fallen ill in the middle of the night, or that a star had forgotten he had another appointment. I learned later that he or she simply refused to get up at an ungodly hour of the morning to do a radio show.

The first time someone chickened out I called Mitzi Green and cried, "Help me. So-and-so can't make it this morning. I have no guest, and I don't know what to do."

Mitzi's big mistake was agreeing to come right over that very first time. Thereafter, whenever someone didn't show, it was Mitzi I called on for help. And every time I called on her she came through. One day she came on as Katharine Hepburn. Another time as Margaret Sullavan. Once she was both Ethel Barrymore and George Arliss. The FCC rules in those days were not as stringent about truthtelling as they are

9

now. If they were, I certainly didn't know about it. The announcer and engineer in the booth aided and abetted our fraud and never once told the manager of the station that so many of these big stars were, in reality, the very best friend I had in the world, Mitzi Green. I had more big-name celebs come on at the last minute for free than any other radio show in New York. Most of those names were, of course, impersonations done by Mitzi Green.

# I Do and I Did!

It was through Mitzi Green that I met Nancy Kelly. Nancy, still in her teens, was then under contract with Twentieth Century-Fox and had already co-starred with Tyrone Power and Henry Fonda in *Jesse James* and with Spencer Tracy in *Stanley and Livingston*.

Nancy's Hollywood career took off after she appeared on Broadway as Gertrude Lawrence's daughter in *Susan and God*. After that she went to Hollywood under contract to Twentieth Century-Fox.

When I met Nancy, she was starring on Broadway in a play called *Flare Path*. Playing opposite her was an English actor new to this country named Alec Guinness.

It's a wonder Nancy and I ever became close friends, because the very first time, through Mitzi, she promised to come on my radio program, but never showed up! When I arrived home from the studio that afternoon, I found the apartment filled with flowers—all of them sent with separate notes of apology from Nancy Kelly. You couldn't stay angry at someone *that* sorry—so, instead, we became good friends.

Like Mitzi, Nancy's big mistake was becoming my friend, because from then on I had two people I could call at the last minute to replace a "no show" guest on my radio show. Nancy commuted back and forth from Hollywood, making movies there, returning to New York to do the then-top-rated TV shows like "Studio One," or "Playhouse 90."

Several years later, Nancy Kelly was there when my husband proposed to me.

I met Army Lieutenant Edward James Slotkin, who was home on leave from Alaska, on a blind date, arranged for by his sister, Selma. Not having seen females other than Eskimo women for about two years, he fell in love with the first girl he met on his return to the States. Happily, that was me.

I went out with him every night for the ten nights of his ten-day leave. The eighth night was New Year's Eve. Naturally, he expected me to spend it with him. In those days girls always made dates for New Year's Eve a year in advance because it was total disgrace and humiliation to spend that night dateless.

Well, I had made my date with Henry H., Jr., months before. I considered myself lucky because he was mighty handsome.

Edward's family was giving a New Year's Eve party in honor of their son who had been away in the Army for three and one-half years. I promised Edward I would show up at the Slotkin house with my date sometime during the evening.

I had, however, also promised Nancy Kelly to pick her up at the airport that same night; she was arriving from Hollywood at 8 P.M.

The plane was delayed and poor Henry H., Jr., had to sit around the airport in a tuxedo until 11 P.M. when Nancy finally arrived.

And the plans Henry originally had made for that night had to be scratched because when we finally got Nancy and her luggage into Henry's car, dropped her luggage off at the Sherry-Netherland Hotel, I announced that we had to drop in at a party. Naturally, it was the Slotkin party. By now Henry was barely talking to me. It didn't matter because I felt the really important guy in my life was about to be Lieutenant Edward James Slotkin. It was wartime and we all lived via ration stamps, so you can imagine how exciting it was to see a long dining-room table sagging under the weight of roast beefs, hams, turkeys, hot dogs and fillets of beef.

True, Edward's father, Samuel Slotkin, was chairman of the Board and president of Hygrade Food Products Corporation. But just as true was the fact (later learned) that the Slotkins had saved all their meat stamps for months ahead and had also borrowed some from friends in order to celebrate their son's short leave.

Henry H., Jr., was the only unhappy guest at the party. He kept wanting to go on to the other places where we had been expected much earlier. The Slotkins' apartment was large enough to accommodate comfortably the hundreds of guests milling around the rooms, yet the only place where Edward could talk to me, without a lot of people snooping, was in the master bathroom.

Knowing that Nancy Kelly was my close friend, he insisted she join us in the bathroom. There, in the least likely romantic spot and in front of Nancy Kelly, Edward asked me to marry him. How many girls do you know have been proposed to in a john? I ought to try that out on "I've Got a Secret!"

Edward explained that he would have to go back to Alaska in a couple of days, but fully expected to be rotated back to the States in the near future.

"We can get married then," he said.

The whole idea was very exciting. But first things first. There was the matter of my very angry date, who wanted now only to get me home. And I couldn't blame him. Edward wouldn't budge from that bathroom until I promised to meet him later to give him my answer. Only when I said, "Yes, we'd meet later," did we leave the john.

As soon as he shut the door behind him, Nancy said, "All that meat! Shirley, for God's sake, marry him!"

All around the apartment that night we kept hearing people mumble, "Slotkin—one hundred million dollars, Hygrade—one hundred million dollars." So Nancy exclaimed, "My God, Shirley, all that meat and one hundred million dollars too. How can you turn him down?" All I kept saying was "Yeah, and besides that, he's good-looking!"

Suddenly there was a loud pounding on the door. It was my date telling us he was going home with or without us! I couldn't blame him for being angry.

Still, he was polite enough to drop Nancy off at her hotel and take me home to my apartment. The only time I saw him smile that night was when he said, "Good night." Actually it was "Good-by," because I never saw or heard from him again.

I called Edward, who picked me up and off we went to a club on 52nd Street called Tony's Wife. That night Tony told us about his beautiful daughter who was studying ballet. (Years later, Tony's daughter married director John Huston.)

On New Year's Day I told my parents about the proposal I had received from the lieutenant. I told them about the groaning food table filled with meats. I also told them that the Slotkins had one hundred million dollars. I explained that I knew about the hundred million because everyone at the party kept talking about it. Even though it was an interesting subject, I had never before heard a host's fortune discussed that openly before. It was definitely bad manners, and terribly *de trop*.

My father looked at me as if he had sired an idiot. He opened *The New York Times* to the financial pages and pointed to the year-end statement of Hygrade Food Products. Then he patiently explained, because I didn't understand financial statements, that it was the first year Hygrade had reached the hundred-million mark in sales. And that's what all the guests at the party were discussing, which had nothing to do with the personal wealth of the Slotkin family. It was a victory for the company.

Well, once I understood it, I tried to tell Nancy Kelly on the phone about the difference, but she still insisted Edward had to have part of that in his pocket. True, he did spend a lot of loot each time we went out. But he told me later that he could afford it because he had been a big winner at poker during all those months cooped up with the guys in Alaska. When the weather went way below zero, it was either poker and/or chess—that's all there was!

Edward went back to Alaska for another two months. Four days after he returned in 1944 to be stationed in the States, we were married by Justice Albert Cohn, Appellate Court Justice of the Supreme Court, a close family friend. He performed the marriage ceremony in front of the living-room fireplace in my parents' apartment.

Mitzi Green and Nancy Kelly were my matrons of honor. Mitzi at the time was married to Joe Pevney, who was away at war; Nancy had been married and divorced from actor Edmond O'Brien. Since neither one of them could be a maid of honor, I had two matrons of honor.

Mitzi was there before 5 P.M., the time set for the ceremony. Nancy was not. At 5:30, my father who definitely was not show-business oriented and who firmly believed in punctuality said, "Since your one matron of honor is here and it is entirely unnecessary to have two, we will begin the marriage ceremony at ONCE!"

Just as Judge Cohn was about to pronounce us man and wife, the doorbell rang and in came matron of honor number two, breathlessly apologizing for being so late. It seems she was out looking for something "special" to give me on my wedding day.

The ceremony halted when she arrived, then continued and Edward and I became man and wife. We don't know what anybody else thought about it, but Edward and I thought Nancy's entrance the funniest thing that had ever happened.

I learned, in the ten days we had gotten to know each other, that Edward was the most adjustable person in the world. He adapted to me and all my friends instantly. When he married me, he knew absolutely nothing about show business. It wasn't too long after, though, that he took out his own subscription to weekly *Variety*. True, he only reads the financial statements of the plays and movies, but, nevertheless, he is a subscriber.

Oh, the present Nancy so desperately wanted me to have on my wedding day was a floor-length pink maribou negligee. It was something Joan Crawford might have worn in a plush MGM movie. I wore it sometimes over my favorite going-to bed outfit—the tops of Edward's pajamas.

# Dining with the Best

Every once in a while when I'm dining at the posh "21" Club, I recall with amusement and some embarrassment the first time I stepped foot in that famous restaurant.

Mitzi Green, in her teens at the time (as was I), asked me to lunch, saying, "The treat's on me. Where would you like to go?"

I thought of the many glamorous places I had read about in the Broadway columns and "21" seemed to be the most exciting. However, I was certain it would be a bore to Mitzi because after all, as a celebrity, she dined there all the time. But, hoping she wouldn't mind, I said, "21."

It was a hot summer day, and my linen dress was pretty wrinkled by the time I got to "21." Mitzi had been out doing errands since early that morning so she wasn't exactly fresh either. Mitzi, who had been waiting for me inside said, "Our table is upstairs."

Now upstairs at "21" has several rooms. It you are a "21" regular you are apt to sit in the front room. If you are not known, you are probably given a table (at least you were then) in one of the back rooms. Mind you, these back rooms are just as beautiful, and some

17

celebrities prefer them. Not being versed at the time on restaurant-table hierarchy, I figured "dis must be da place." After all, Mitzi Green was a famous star.

We sat at our table talking away until someone came to take the drink order. Neither one of us drank, but neither one of us had the guts to confess this to the formidable maitre d'. So we each ordered a glass of sherry. In movies, properly bred ladies always drank sherry.

A bus boy, carrying a gigantic covered silver roll-top tray via a strap around his neck, kept stopping at our table so we could choose the hot breads, rolls and/ or muffins we wanted to eat.

I couldn't understand how Mitzi managed to keep her svelte figure because every time that boy passed the table, she stopped him and piled her bread-and-butter plate with his goodies.

Then the maitre d' came with the long menu. I observed that the prices were definitely higher than Hamburger Heaven (my usual place for lunching), but I figured it couldn't possibly matter to "big star" Mitzi Green.

To this day I can still remember that I ordered shrimp first, a sunset salad as the main course and a fruit compote for dessert. Mitzi perused the menu, then looked the frock-coated maitre d' straight in the eye and said, "I'm not very hungry. When Miss Eder gets to dessert, you can bring me a fruit compote, too."

For a gal who wasn't hungry, she sure was hung up on bread.

During the many courses of my lunch, she ate some bran muffins, eleven toasted hard rolls with butter and six pieces of melba toast. I offered her a taste of shrimp and some of my salad, but she still insisted she wasn't hungry.

When it was time for dessert, the waiter, without much flair (how much flair can accompany a fruit compote?), set the fruit-filled dishes down before us.

He also set down at each place, a large spoon. I held the spoon up to Mitzi and said, "Would you believe that a fancy place like this could make the mistake of serving a soup spoon with dessert? I've never heard of such a thing, have you?"

Mitzi said, "Let's show it to the maitre d', he'll be shocked. Waiter," she called in her most professional voice. The waiter came, but not the maitre d'.

"Please ask that little man in the frock coat to come to our table," she told him.

He came at once, solicitously asking, "Is there anything wrong?"

"I'll say there is," exclaimed Mitzi. "How come a place as fancy as '21' serves soup spoons when there is no soup on the table?"

"Madam," replied the maitre d' in his best imitation of Arthur Treacher, "those are dessert spoons."

If only we could have died on the spot!

After eating the fruit with the "soup spoons," Mitzi asked for her check. It came to sixteen dollars without the tip. Sixteen dollars then was equal to about thirty dollars today and even then, it was a heck of a lot of money for teen-agers to spend for lunch—even if one was starring in a Broadway play.

Going down the stairs toward the door, Mitzi was recognized by several people and she was asked to sign autographs. (Aside from being in *Babes in Arms,* Mitzi Green had been a famous child star in movies.)

Peter Kriendler, a member of the famed Kriendler family, who along with Charlie Berns owned "21," saw Mitzi, kissed her on the cheek and said, "I didn't know you were here. Why didn't somebody tell me?"

I suppose he meant had he been told, we would have been seated in the front room. Thinking back, I'm sure we would have been doubly humiliated in the front room over dessert.

When we got out into the street, Mitzi turned to me and said, "Shirley, I'm hungry. Will you come to Schrafft's while I get something to eat?"

It was only then that Mitzi admitted to me that she had never before been to "21." And it seems that when she looked at the prices on the menu she realized she only had enough money with her for *one* of us to eat!

Talk about giggling teen-agers. We giggled all the way to Schrafft's, and we often laughed about it, from that day on through the many years of our friendship —a friendship that continued until the day she died in her forties from cancer.

And you know something? Somewhere (wherever it is), you can bet that from time to time Mitzi is still laughing.

# A Tough Chapter to Write

Writing about the passing of a close friend is a difficult task. Mitzi Green was truly one of the most beloved people in show business. Some of you may remember her as a child star, when she was Becky Thatcher to Jackie Coogan's Tom Sawyer. Others remember her bringing Broadway audiences to their feet with "bravos" each time she sang "The Lady Is a Tramp," "Where or When" and "Funny Valentine" in the Rodgers and Hart musical *Babes in Arms*.

Many performers have been credited with introducing these songs, but it was Mitzi who first stopped shows cold with them. She was the very first big star I knew well.

I went on to college, and Mitzi, after *Babes in Arms*, went on to become a top night-club performer; appearing in New York at the Copacabana, in Detroit at the Bowery or the DAC, at the Cocoanut Grove in Los Angeles, the Riviera in Vegas and on and on.

Mitzi Green was one of the greatest mimics or impressionists in the business. Even today, the only two on a par with her are Frank Gorshin and Rich Little. Audiences adored her impressions of Ethel Barrymore and Joe E. Lewis singing "Cement Mixer Putty Putty" to each other. Whenever I sent her the SOS, she'd come on with me and right there on the show we'd have Ed Wynn, or Fanny Brice or Sophie Tucker.

The real Fanny Brice used to say, if ever her life story was done on the screen, she wanted only Mitzi Green to play her. It didn't work out that way. A youngster by the name of Barbra Streisand made her mark in show business starring in *Funny Girl*, the story of Fanny Brice.

Mitzi married an actor-director, who at the time was a soldier, named Joseph Pevney. My father married them in his chambers. They wanted to keep it very hush hush. It was, until I announced it on the air minutes after the ceremony. Mitzi and Joe were not as angry with me as my father, who was furious because I had violated a confidence.

When Joe Pevney came back from overseas and got out of service, he went to Hollywood to become a director of motion pictures. It was Joe who helped Debbie Reynolds to stardom in *Tammy* and pushed Tony Curtis and Jeff Chandler up by their novice-actor bootstraps.

Mitzi really preferred being Mrs. Joseph Pevney and mother of their three sons and one daughter to performing. She came out of retirement only now and then to do a Milton Berle or an Ed Sullivan TV show.

Often she laughingly apologized to my parents, and later to my husband, for aiding and abetting my career in show business.

Mitzi was the direct product of show-business parents whose popular vaudeville act was known across the U.S.A. as "Keno and Green." When Mitzi was about three, she simply strolled out onto the stage during one performance, and did an imitation of the star act on the bill, which was "Moran and Mack." That did it! Her overjoyed parents, Rosie and Joe, melted into the background and pushed their talented daughter right into the spotlight.

In 1961, Mitzi did a short tour in *Gypsy* and in it

also was her twelve-year-old son Jeff. At the time, Jeff thought he wanted to be an actor. After the tour, he changed his mind.

Mitzi dear, thank you for always being right there to help me when I needed your help. Oh, I can see you now, shaking your head, laughing and saying, "Shirl—I'm sorry I did it to you." I'm not sorry, Mitzi Green, I'm grateful. But I'm even more grateful just for having known you.

# Hatbox Caper

Years and years ago, when I was a new bride, my husband had to go on business to Providence, Rhode Island, from New York, where we then lived. Knowing Providence was close to Boston, I asked to go along because a friend of mine, a young important actress, was trying out a new play in Boston opposite John Garfield.

I called my friend and told her I would be taking a train at 6 A.M. from Providence, arriving at the Ritz Hotel about seven o'clock the same morning. My husband would come in about 8 P.M. to have dinner and see the play. Then we'd take the overnight train back to New York.

My friend, who must remain nameless for obvious reasons, said, "Good. When the train gets in, come right to the hotel. Leave your things in my room. We'll have breakfast together, and you can sit in my dressing room during the matinee."

I arrived on schedule at the Ritz Hotel, carrying a Sally Victor hatbox. I knocked on the door of her room. She didn't answer. Knowing she liked to sleep late in the morning, I figured she didn't hear the first knock, so I pounded the door hard. Pretty soon it opened—just a crack—and a sleepy-looking actress mumbled, "Oh, my God, I forgot you were coming."

"Well, here I am," I exclaimed, bubbling over with anticipation.

"Yes, here you are," she parroted lamely. I tried to push my way in through the small crack, but I couldn't make it, although my Sally Victor hatbox did.

"Look," said my friend, "why don't you go downstairs and wait in the lobby until I brush my teeth and put on some clothes?"

"How long do I have to wait?" I asked angrily; I had gotten up at 5 A.M. to ride a six o'clock milk train into Boston just to see her.

"Come back in an hour," she mumbled and slammed the door shut. I was boiling mad. How dare she tell me to go sit in the lobby for an hour? But, where does one go in Boston at seven o'clock in the morning? What's more, there wasn't even a coffee shop.

I just sat in a straight-backed chair in the lobby of the Ritz, thinking all the time, "I'll have to go back upstairs again, because I have nowhere else to go until Edward arrives tonight." I was very young and totally inexperienced in making travel arrangements, or I might have gone back to New York.

When the clock in the lobby said eight o'clock I went back up to her room, prepared with a fully rehearsed nasty speech. This time when I knocked, she opened the door wide and said "Come in, Shirley." She was freshly made up, and wearing a robe. As I entered the room, almost stumbling over the Sally Victor hatbox, I saw a man in bed. I recognized him right away. It was John (known to his intimates as Julie) Garfield. An old cliché maybe, but if the earth could have opened up and swallowed me, I would have said, "Thank you, God!"

"Hi," said the familiar voice as he sat up in bed. My friend by now had disappeared into the bathroom. I can't even remember if I said hello.

"Sit down," he said, patting the edge of the bed. I

25

don't remember answering that either. I just kept my eyes fixed on the Sally Victor hatbox on the floor.

"If you turn around," said the famous movie star, "I can get out of bed and get dressed. You see, I have nothing on."

I do, indeed, remember immediately turning around.

"Does this shock you?" asked John (Julie) Garfield. "I understand you've only been married a short time. But, after all, you *are* married."

Yeah, I was married, but until the night of my wedding and maybe even for some time after, I thought babies came from sitting on a cold stoop. (That's because my mother told me never to sit on a stoop with a boy after a date.)

"You can turn around now," said the fully clothed Garfield. I did. "Don't blame so-and-so. She wanted me to leave before you came back upstairs. It was all my doing. You see, she told me about your sheltered background, and I thought it would be an eye opener for you to know that there is another side of life."

It was an eye opener all right! It took me some ten years to be able to shut them without the sight of a naked, from the waist up (blankets covered him to there), John-Julie Garfield. My friend, who was obviously embarrassed, stayed in the bathroom until I left the room with Mr. Garfield. He to go back to his own quarters in the hotel, and I to go back down to the lobby to sit in that straight-backed chair possibly for seven hours until my husband arrived from Providence.

When Edward did arrive, we had dinner, went to see the play, and went backstage to visit my friend as if nothing had happened. That was the night I became a master at small talk, especially when John Garfield joined us for supper after the show. Before we left to catch the midnight train home, I even called him "Julie." After all, I knew him well enough, didn't I?

I was so embarrassed about the day's adventure I

didn't tell my husband the true story until five years later, figuring by then I knew *him* well enough. He laughed hard and long. We laugh about it today, when we see John Garfield movies on the "late show."

It took me a long while to look my friend in the eye again, but I did. We are still good friends. Recently, when I mentioned that I had to go to the Ritz Hotel in Boston to review a play, she said, "Don't forget to take a Sally Victor hatbox with you. If you can't get in—it will."

# Disaster on TV

Long before she became a best-selling author, Jacqueline Susann did TV commercials and was also "fem-cee" of an early TV game show on the Dumont network called "Ring the Bell."

The panel of "experts" was made up of major and minor celebrities who, if they gave the correct answer to the first question, won something like a toaster; for the second question, the prize may have been a dinner for two at a restaurant; for the third correct answer, the participant would receive something equally as inconsequential. The fourth and final prize was a specified amount of cash, which meant the fourth and final prize question was a toughie. If a panelist gave an incorrect answer, a bell went off which automatically eliminated him from the show.

Because Jackie Susann was my friend and knew I was dying to get on a TV show—any show—she managed to talk the producer into having me on "Ring the Bell." At the time, my only claim to fame was the fact that I had a column in several weekly newspapers in New York.

Since this was my TV debut, you can be sure I had my mother, father and every living relative and/or friend (close or otherwise), watching "Ring the Bell." I also put a tag at the end of one of my weekly columns telling all the readers to be sure and see it. For those who didn't own TV sets, I suggested they go to the nearest bar to watch.

I arrived at the Dumont studios to be greeted by Jackie, who took me aside to explain the rules. This was before the FCC blew the whistle on the "$64,000 Question," so the rules were not very stringent. As a matter of fact, each of us was given a piece of paper with the answers to questions for numbers one and two, just so we wouldn't look stupid. For answers to numbers three and four, we were on our own, but knowing the answers to the first two enabled us to stay on camera for at least ten minutes of the half-hour show.

A few minutes before air time we were all placed in chairs behind a desk which had a high ledge in front. Roddy McDowall was on the show that day, I remember. Behind this ledge, where no viewer could peek, we placed the answers or notes to the first two questions.

The questions were so easy I didn't even bother to glance at the answers.

A man named Hal Tunis was the moderator. As I sat there smiling so that my relatives, friends and readers could see how self-assured I was, I heard Mr. Tunis say "And first we call on Shirley Eder. Shirley, give us the name of three states beginning with A." Loud and clear with great projection I said, right into the camera with the little red light, "Atlanta."

The bell went off, and I heard either Miss Susann or Mr. Tunis say, "Wrong! I'm sorry, but Shirley Eder you are eliminated from the game!"

"Wrong?" How could I be wrong? Too late I glanced down at the answer in front of me and saw that indeed Atlanta was not a state beginning with A. It wasn't a state at all! My first appearance on television and my big break lasted less than thirty seconds! That was heartbreaking in itself, but what was worse, I had to go home and face my parents, relatives, friends and readers. And, would you believe, not until the show was over did I understand that I flunked because Atlanta is a city and not a state!

I cannot tell you how many times since, over dinner together at Danny's Hideaway, or "21" or at the Beverly Hills Hotel, Jacqueline Susann says, "Shirley, name three states beginning with A."

When I went with Bob Hope on his last Christmas tour to Asia, someone from his office called to tell me where we would be going. Later when I told my family about it I said I couldn't remember, but I knew it was in Thailand and it began with a "B." Then I said, "It must be Burma." My son, John, patiently explained that it couldn't be Burma because Burma was not in Thailand. By process of elimination they discovered that it was Bangkok. So you see, I haven't progressed much in geography!

# Vic Damone

Thinking back to when Vic Damone was a young hot record seller even before he went into the Army, a mutual friend made an appointment for me to interview him on the thirtieth floor of the RCA Building on Decoration Day. If you can picture that huge Rockefeller Center skyscraper with maybe just one office open and no one in the building except one elevator man, Vic Damone and yours truly, you have a picture that resembles the last scene from the movie *On the Beach*.

As I got off the elevator the only noise I heard except the clicking of my heels was music coming from somewhere down the hall. It had to be our rendezvous place simply because the music was a Vic Damone record. There in an office with the door open was the young Italian singer (I can't recall if he was wearing his old or new nose at the time), standing next to a record player that was playing a not yet released Damone record called "Happy Feet."

"Hi," he said, "listen to this new record." I did. Then he played a few more Vic Damone records—some new, some old. After a twenty-minute concert, I looked at my watch. At home, there was waiting for me in our Washington Square apartment a husband and a three-month-old daughter.

"Oh," exclaimed Damone, "I guess you want to get to the interview. Let's sit over here," he said patting the couch. I had a feeling I shouldn't be sitting on that couch with "Mr. Wonderful." But there I was—so I asked questions. He answered them. Pretty soon I felt an arm creeping around my shoulder. Since there were only two of us in the room and I'm not double jointed . . . Immature thoughts began to surface such as: "What do I do if his other hand comes around and stops, God knows where? If I scream, who will hear me in this deserted tower of glass and steel?"

Just as panic set in, Damone looked into my eyes and said, "I've always admired older women!" That did it! True, Damone was younger, but I was only in my early twenties. No longer giving a damn, I stood up and said, "I have to get home to my husband and child." Gallantly he offered to drive me home. I thanked him for the offer "but, no thanks."

Out on the street I searched in vain for a taxi. Try and get a taxi in New York on a sunny holiday afternoon—the cab drivers are all out with their families looking for cabs.

Some twenty minutes later while still shouting, "Taxi," a sleek convertible Cadillac with the top down (naturally) came up in front of me and the driver said, "Taxi, ma'am." You're right, it was Vic Damone. By then I would have been grateful for a lift from Dracula. All the way down from Fiftieth Street to 37 Washington Square West, I kept talking about my "wonderful" husband and beautiful child. Maybe I exaggerated a little, but I felt compelled to keep talking about them for two reasons: one, to make sure he knew I was a married lady, and the other because I found young Mr. Damone very attractive!

When we arrived at the apartment house Vic said,

"I'd like to meet your husband." I felt safe enough here to say, "Sure, come on up."

Vic went to park the car. Smugly I said to the doorman, "Would you call my apartment and tell my husband I am coming up with Vic Damone?" As we walked to the elevator the doorman called: "Your husband is visiting in the Nathanson apartment."

Mrs. Nathanson happened to be singing star Carol Bruce who, at the time, was starring on Broadway in *Show Boat.* Since the elevator was already on its way up, there was no time to give my friend and neighbor Carol Bruce advance warning of our visit. We definitely were going to stop there to pick up my husband.

I rang her bell. The door was opened by an apparition in a cold-creamed face and hair that was wound around Toilet-paper rollers. Carol Bruce took one look at Vic Damone, screamed, "Oh, my God!" and slammed the door shut.

I just had to get in. My husband was in there! I rang the bell again. This time the door was opened by Edward who, like a friendly puppy, shook hands with Damone, saying, "Carol refuses to let you in and I'm in the middle of a gin hand with Milton (her husband). Here's the key to our apartment," he said, tossing it to me. "Take Mr. Damone up and I'll be there soon." Again the door closed. By now Mr. Damone had had it. The sight of such ugly domesticity turned him off—but good. He looked at his watch, as I had looked at mine earlier in his office, and said, "Golly, I just remembered an appointment. I'm sure if you ring the bell again, they'll let you in if I'm not here!" We shook hands good-by, and not even bothering to wait for the elevator, off he went walking down fifteen floors!

As of this writing, Vic Damone has been married three times. I have often wondered how he ever married even once after that day!

Fade out the late 1940s. Fade in the late 1960s

and another interview. This time with a balding but still handsome Vic Damone. Maybe now I might have been slightly more receptive to his amorous advances, but they weren't offered this time.

# So Long, New York

A born and bred New Yorker dreads having to leave the city to live anywhere else in the U.S.A. And when and if the time comes to do so, take it from one who knows—you feel as though you are going to "Nowhere U.S.A."

It takes time, after you leave it, to learn that New York is really just a hick town with a swollen ego.

How do I know all this? Well, when my father-in-law, my husband and my brother-in-law decided to move the head offices of their company, Hygrade Food Products, to Detroit, Michigan, I found out.

I fought off the move for two years, which meant my husband had to commute back and forth from Detroit to New York. Then, I had to make the decision. Did I want to keep his love or the love I had for my native city? It actually came down to that. My husband, Edward, threatened to leave me for good if I didn't pick up our two kids and make the move—at once (after all, it had been two years of commuting for him).

Even though I felt leaving New York was going over a precipice into nowhere, I knew I'd go with him, because just like it says in that song: "A good man is hard to find."

What was I going to do without New York City and what was New York City going to do without me? Well, it's been a lot of years now and amazingly enough both New York and I have done very well without each other.

I didn't make the decision to go to Detroit entirely by myself. I remember going to my father and asking him just what my rights in the matter were. Did I really have to move because of my husband's business?

My father's exact words were: "As a justice of the state of New York, I can assure you that you have absolutely no rights. If a husband is willing to support a wife, she must go wherever he earns his living. If she does not go, she is not entitled to a single cent of support. Speaking, not as a judge but as your father, if you don't make plans to move immediately, your mother and I will advise your husband to divorce you. What's more, I will be his witness in court."

Would you believe parents could do this to an only child?!

Well, it was official! We were moving from 29 Washington Square West to a place that majored in assembly lines. Why it was important for a meat-packing company to be based in Detroit I could not understand at the time.

So there began a round of farewell parties for Shirley and Ed.

One that stands out vividly in my mind was given for us by columnist Earl Wilson and his B.W., Rosemary. Every VIP in New York (whether we knew him or not) was invited to bid us farewell. About a week before the party, Rosemary Wilson called to ask if we minded sharing honors with Lilo, who was leaving the cast of the Cole Porter hit *Can-Can*. Could I say "no" to Rosemary? We would just have to go halvies on the guests of honor bit.

What the heck, it wouldn't be too bad sharing honors with Lilo. After all, she had been the toast of Broadway for a couple of seasons.

Lilo and her husband, the Marquis Guy de la Passardiere, and the Edward Slotkins arrived downstairs at the Wilsons' apartment house at the same time. The Marquis was carrying an enormous something from the cab.

He explained that it was a large painting (which I couldn't see because it was covered with a velvet cloth). As a matter of fact, my husband helped him carry the painting into the elevator.

We had already sent the Wilsons a "thank you" present for the party, but I was sure it was nothing quite so lavish as what the Passardieres were lugging in. I mean, how could you compare one case of hot dogs, a five-pound salami and a dozen steaks to a Renoir or a Dufy?

Once inside the Wilson apartment, as Edward and I began to greet friends, I noticed that Lilo and her spouse had disappeared from sight. When I asked Earl where they were, he said they were in the dining room hanging the painting.

I whispered to Edward that I definitely would go to Cartier's the next day to send another, more lavish, thank you gift. Instead of having to keep up with the Joneses, we had to keep up with French nobility.

When it was announced that we could now go into the dining room to choose our food from the buffet, my heart sank. This meant it was also time for everyone to view the Rembrandt or Picasso which was being given to the hosts by the coguests of honor.

The dining-room doors opened. Purposely I lagged behind three Gabors, the Joey Adamses, Virginia Graham, Jacqueline Susann and Diana Dors etc., etc. Still, from the dining room I could hear all the "oohs" and "aahs" as the guests glommed the painting.

Finally we just *had* to go into the dining room. We

went in—looked up—and then I laughed like crazy, mostly from relief.

After I saw it, I knew I wouldn't have to go to Cartier's the next day. The hot dogs, salami and steaks we sent the Wilsons were okay.

Hanging on the wall of the Wilsons' dining room was a six-foot-tall portrait of Lilo, which had just been completed. She was unveiling the painting at the party which was being given "half" in her honor.

I begged my husband to rush down to Washington Square to bring up the portrait which had been done of me at age ten. I wanted equal time. He refused to go, even though I accused him of not having a sense of humor.

When all the other guests departed and it was time for the multiple guests of honor to go too, the Marquis and Lilo took her portrait off the wall, covered it with the velvet cloth and home they went, to hang it in their own apartment.

We wouldn't think of taking our hot dogs, salamis and steaks home with us. And you know, it's just as proper to hang a salami as it is a painting!

# Motor City, Here We Come

Before we left for our new home in Detroit, we were wined and dined and partied by our friends in New York. (We weren't too sure if we were given all these parties because they were sad or glad to see us go.)

*I* was plenty sad, that's for sure. Nevertheless, we gave the final farewell bash, which took place on the enormous terrace of my parents' penthouse. I suppose if our party were given somewhere other than in New York City it would have been called a cook-out.

There was music and dancing. For some reason (I can't remember why), I insisted on having Hungarian gypsy music, which necessitated the musicians bringing their piano-size zimbalon with them. My parents wouldn't permit us to drag their baby grand out onto the terrace.

Among the 150 guests were Shirley Booth, Lena Horne, the Robert Sterlings (Anne Jeffreys), the Earl Wilsons, Mimi Benzell, Lilo and her Marquis, the McGuire Sisters, Marion Marlowe, Kaye (her name still had the "e" at the end then) Ballard, Eva Gabor, Janet Blair, Carol Bruce and others who must forgive me for not remembering. They know I was under a terrific emotional strain at the time because I was leaving the "only" city in the U.S.A.

Eva Gabor arrived with the best-looking young man. She introduced him as Efrem Zimbalist.

The gypsy music was loud enough to attract a large number of people down in the street, and when we looked over the side of the terrace on this beautiful spring night, we saw dozens of people on the street looking up to see where the gypsies were camping out.

As Miss Gabor and Mr. Zimbalist danced by the musicians, the leader kept bowing to Mr. Zimbalist.

"Ah ha!" I thought. "This must be the famous musician Efrem Zimbalist. But how young he looks to be so world famous and for so many years!"

The music was infectious. Guests sang from their tables. Others got up to dance either by themselves or with partners. Some, even in groups.

Mimi Benzell sang "Musetta's Waltz" from *La Bohème*. Mimi had been considered a star at the Metropolitan Opera until Rudolph Bing took over and decided to make an example of her by dismissing her from the roster of the Met because she accepted engagements to sing in supper clubs.

Subsequently, she sued Mr. Bing and the Metropolitan Opera, claiming he had caused her grief and loss of work. The suit lingered on in the courts for years.

My mother, seeing Efrem Zimbalist, said, "I don't know the name of that handsome young man, but I watch him every day on a TV soap opera."

Scoffingly I asked, "How could the famous concert violinist Efrem Zimbalist appear on a daily TV soap opera?" He looked so young I was positive he had taken some of those famous Swiss rejuvenation shots. This didn't deter my mother from insisting she saw this man on television daily! If he wasn't *the* Zimbalist how come the musicians kept bowing to him all evening long?

To prove my point, I went over to Mimi Benzell

and said, "Aren't you thrilled to have sung tonight for the great Zimbalist?"

Mimi, pointing to the dreamy-looking young man, said, "Oh, you mean Efrem? We've known each other since we were kids. I've often sung for his father, Efrem Zimbalist, Senior."

You see, Efrem, Jr., had not yet become a star. Few people recognized him. I certainly had never seen him before. But why should the musicians keep bowing if he wasn't *the* Zimbalist?

This puzzled me enough to go over to the orchestra leader and ask him if they know this Mr. Zimbalist.

"I have known him," said the leader, "for many years. I played for parties at his father's home with my orchestra. We have all known Efrem, Jr., since he was a small boy. And just six months ago we played for his sister's wedding. Efrem, Jr., you know, now acts on a daily soap opera."

Why is it my mother is always right? Why is every mother always right?

One of my very best friends is lyricist-composer Lyn Duddy. Lyn and his partner Joan Edwards (who was, for years the star of the Lucky Strike Hit Parade) wrote special material to sing at the party.

Lyn later partnered with Jerry Bresler to write some of the best musical acts in the business, including Robert Goulet's record-breaking one at the Plaza, right after he closed in *Camelot*. They write most of Totie Fields's special songs and wrote all the music and lyrics for Jackie Gleason's "Honeymooners" on TV.

Anyway, Lyn Duddy and Joan Edwards somehow managed to get most of the stars at the party to sing their material about our leave-taking from New York.

Even though the lyrics were funny, some of them made me cry, especially the words they wrote to the tune of Jule Styne's "Bye Bye, Baby" from *Gentlemen Prefer Blondes* which went:

*Bye, Bye, Shirley*
*Remember you're our girlie*
*When you get to Detroit*
*You're leaving first nights in Ermine*
*And stars you've adored*
*Good-by, Ethel Merman*
*Hello, Henry Ford!*
*Please take warning*
*Noel and Cole have gone in mourning*
*Poor Manhattan could cry*
*But even though we may part*
*You've claimed a million hearts*
*From which you'll never say, 'Bye, Bye!'*

Everyone else laughed. I sobbed.

Lena Horne sang. So did Shirley Booth and Carol Bruce. It was a gay night for everyone, except me.

Vincent Sardi, Jr., was at the party too. Would I ever again be considered a regular at Sardi's? Probably not. My whole glamorous life was over. No one from show business, I thought, ever came to Detroit. I'd never see Vincent again, or Lena Horne or any of the familiar faces.

The last song sung that night was "The Party's Over," and I burst into tears. It was certainly all over for me—this way of life was finished.

Well, we moved to Detroit. Ten days after we got there my husband had to go back to New York on business, and he felt so sorry for me he took me along. It had only been ten days, but I felt as though I had been banished for ten years.

We went to the theatre that first night back, then over to Sardi's for supper. There was *my* Vincent at the door. I cried out: "Vincent, Vincent, I'm back!"

He looked at me as if I was mad, and said, "Back? I didn't know you had ever gone!" My husband laughed, but I was crushed.

Several months after we moved to our new home in Detroit, Hildegarde came to town to perform at the Statler. We gave our first Detroit party—for Hildegarde. I called Lyn Duddy in New York and asked if he would send some special lyrics the guests could sing to her. He didn't send the lyrics. He and Joan Edwards surprised us by showing up in person with their music and lyrics. With Joan at the piano, they sang their special songs to Hildegarde.

I also remember a young man at the party who was in town to promote his first record album. He was a friend of Lyn's, and not too many of our Detroit friends knew who he was despite the fact that with his brothers he had been a part of Kay Thompson's famous night-club act and had also done all right for himself on the late-night Steve Allen show. Andy Williams was his name.

We have had many, many parties in Detroit since then. And thanks to Lyn Duddy and Joan Edwards and to Jerry Bresler, who never let us down despite their own busy schedules, our parties are pretty spectacular, and Lyn is the catalyst who makes them so super. They also wrote brilliant words and music for the parties we have given for Ethel Merman, Kathryn Grayson, Mitzi Gaynor and Jacqueline Susann.

I cannot tell you how many times they arrive in Detroit just a couple of hours before a party, rush to the piano to pound out some original tunes, then quickly move to the typewriters in the den where they sit down to write special lyrics. When they finish writing, they jump into their dinner jackets, run to wherever it is we are having the party (if it's outside the house), rehearse all the special material with the orchestra, stay just long enough to put on a show— then rush to the airport to catch the last plane out of Detroit to New York. And this last plane is never a direct flight! How's that for friendship?

# Kathryn Grayson

Kathryn Grayson is the only singer I know who never warms up her vocal chords before going out on stage, whether it be in concert with the Pittsburgh Symphony or on Broadway in *Camelot* or before a recording session at a movie studio. Once I asked, "How do you know your voice will be there without testing it with a tiny 'Ma, may, mou?'" "I know it's there," said Katie, "simply because I don't abuse it. I have never smoked and I don't drink."

Katie's voice definitely is always there, but I can't say the same for her lyrics. I shall never forget her New York night-club debut at the Latin Quarter, which has since gone the way of most New York night clubs—over and out! She arrived from Los Angeles the day before the opening to learn that the bags which carried her costumes had been lost in flight. I was nervous about this, her manager was nervous, her sister was nervous, her secretary was nervous, her daughter, Patti-Kate, was nervous and the Latin Quarter was panic-stricken. But Kathryn remained extremely cool and collected and was immediately taken to Brooks, theatrical costumers, where several gowns were to be whipped up for the next

44

night's opening. Naturally, the cost of these gowns was tripled, because seamstresses were put on the job around the clock.

As Kathryn stood on a pedestal in a Brooks fitting room, her manager rushed in saying, "Stop whatever you're doing and come with me to the police station. I've been ordered to have you fingerprinted." Kathryn exclaimed, "I didn't take the bags—they were stolen from me!" We learned it was merely routine procedure in New York City for every night-club performer to be fingerprinted at police headquarters. The next day (the day of the opening night), we went back to Brooks for final fittings with their promise that the costumes would be delivered to the Latin Quarter by 7 P.M. Butterflies flew around my stomach, but Kathryn remained absolutely calm.

"What will you do if the costumes aren't ready on time?" I cried.

"What will I do?" she said. "Either I can kill myself or I go out on stage in my street clothes. Since the choice is up to me, I'll go out in my street clothes!"

Our song bird, who was staying at the Hampshire House, had a hairdressing appointment there at 4 P.M. Mind you, she was due out on that Latin Quarter stage just four hours later. I went with her to the beauty salon for my morale—not for hers. While sitting under the dryer she said, "I can't seem to remember all the words to my opening song 'The Night They Invented Champagne.' Shirl, will you coach me?" So we went over and over the lyrics. Even now I can recite them, but I wouldn't swear the same for Kathryn!

It was now 6 P.M. The still calm Miss Grayson was having her curls combed out. Well, whether or not she knew her lyrics, I had to leave to get dressed, then rush over to the Latin Quarter where we were hosting a large party for my husband's business associates.

Kathryn was due to appear on stage at eight o'clock.

At seven-fifty, her manager came up to our ringside table carrying a sheaf of music which he thrust into my hands. Did this mean she hadn't arrived in time and maybe she expected *me* to go on and recite the music? The little I had eaten began to nudge its way up from the stomach to the throat. Sidney, her manager, said, "Kathryn wants you to hold 'book' for her. And if she forgets a lyric, she expects you to call it out to her."

"She's got to be kidding," I hopefully thought. She wasn't! My husband grabbed the music sheets out of my hand and said, "Not with me here, you won't shout out lyrics from the table!" He knew that if necessary, I just might do it.

The lights dimmed. The orchestra struck up the overture (a medley of songs Kathryn Grayson had introduced in movie musicals). From the wings off-stage, came that beautiful rich voice singing her theme song, "Jealousy." Then, still singing, she strolled onstage. Not, however, in one of the costumes from Brooks. She wore a ball gown I had never seen before. The orchestra began to play "The Night They Invented Champagne."

Stage front, she walked, standing directly over our table smiling down at me with an "I dare you to" look and sang the song from beginning to end. I'd like to say she made no mistakes in the lyrics, but it would be a lie. She sang up such a storm, the audience never noticed. When she finished the number, Kathryn spilled the beans to the audience about the airlines losing her costumes, having new ones made and having to be fingerprinted. And then she said, "For the benefit of my very close friend who is sitting ringside, let me explain that the gown I am wearing is really mine. When I arrived at the club tonight the costumes were hanging up in the dressing room. Beside them were my own, the ones the airlines had mislaid. You see, they recovered them and got them here in time for the opening. And I preferred to open in something

I was familiar with." The audience clapped like crazy for her confession. Then she went into "Un bel di" from *Madama Butterfly,* earning herself a standing ovation. And this was only the middle of her act! She was right not to worry. Obviously, she knew what she was doing all the time. Compared to *Adventures with Kathryn Grayson, The Perils of Pauline* is amateur night.

# Fame Is a Name on a Felt Board

Kathryn Grayson, who followed in Jeanette Mac-Donald's footsteps as MGM's number-one female singing star, was my first real movie-star friend. When I met her she had already been in an Andy Hardy picture with Mickey Rooney (the starting-off point for budding MGM stars), had star billing in *Thousands Cheer,* and had just completed the film *Anchors Aweigh* in which she costarred with Gene Kelly and that skinny kid singer Frank Sinatra.

MGM and Loew's theatres were one corporation before the government stepped in, separating the motion-picture theatres from their film-production companies, and in doing so, helped to almost financially ruin the motion-picture industry. They were able to produce a lot of movies, when by owning theatres, they were sure of product distribution.

Anyway, Metro sent a group of young people east to make personal appearances at their New York City flagship theatre, the Capitol. In that group were Kathryn Grayson, Nancy Walker, June Allyson, Rags Ragland and the already well-known comedian Lou Holtz.

At the time, I had a radio show and was still going to school. The show gave me the privilege of tagging

48

along with the group as they made pre-Capitol one-shot appearances on the stages of Loew's theatres in Brooklyn, Manhattan and the Bronx. During that strenuous one-day tour, I sat next to Kathryn Grayson in the limousine; I had met Nancy Walker before.

At the end of that tour, the weary troupe stopped off backstage at the Capitol to pick up their dressing-room keys prior to opening there the next morning. Kathryn was given the key to dressing room No. 1. June Allyson and Nancy Walker, who had worked together in the stage hit *Best Foot Forward* before going on to Hollywood to re-create their same roles on the screen, were assigned the next dressing rooms. It was Nancy Walker, though, who, in both the stage and screen versions, made the more significant impression on audiences. The room assignments were preissued by the studio in California. And it was obvious the MGM powers knew they had a winner in Kathryn Grayson, which assured her being given dressing room number one. June Allyson and Nancy Walker were given side-by-side dressing rooms, although I don't think there was love lost between them. The word was out to start giving June the "star" treatment because a movie called *Two Girls and a Sailor*, starring June, Gloria De Haven and Van Johnson, had just been previewed and all the audience cards raved about this newcomer. Apparently Louis B. Mayer and all of his "yes" men (were there any "no" men?) realized June's potential as a future star.

June, at the time, was going with a young soldier, but during the long Capitol engagement, she began seeing actor Dick Powell.

The movie then playing the Capitol Theatre was *A Guy Named Joe*, starring Spencer Tracy. The combination of a hit movie and the stage show was so successful, it was held over for seven weeks. Many times the troupe on stage performed seven shows a day. It was definitely a blockbuster, with the paying customers standing in line at the box office from early morning until late at night.

From that very first day when we rode together in the limo, Katie and I have been close friends. Over the years I have often visited her in California. When she was busy making pictures at MGM and I was in California, she'd take me to the studio with her.

During the making of the movie *Show Boat,* in which she starred with Howard Keel, Ava Gardner, Joe E. Brown and Marge and Gower Champion, she took me from the set to the building which housed the female star dressing rooms. Each star under contract on the Metro lot could have her dressing room decorated exactly as she liked. I'm sure the male stars had the same privilege, but, alas, I never saw any of their rooms.

As we entered the building, I saw a large felt board with the names in movable white letters. On that same board I noticed indentations of names who once were superstars at MGM, but were no longer under contract. Among the indented names were Jeanette MacDonald, Myrna Loy, Joan Crawford, Greta Garbo, Ann Sothern—all stars still—but for one reason or another, no longer with Metro.

In white letters I read the names of Kathryn Grayson, June Allyson, Lana Turner, Ava Gardner, Margaret O'Brien, Esther Williams. Those were the *now* stars at that time.

I remember turning to Katie as we entered the building and saying, "Hey—one day, you too will be an indentation." I said it in jest. Katie laughed with me, thinking as I did, it could never happen to her. After all, she called Louis B. Mayer "Pops." I wonder, if all those indentations once called him "Pops" too?

After Mr. Mayer was replaced as the High Lama at Metro by Dore Schary, a young man Mayer personally had helped along in the business, Kathryn asked to be released from her contract. She wanted to freelance. Actors were beginning to get salaries plus a percentage of the picture. You couldn't do this while still under the old studio contracts. It was the beginning of the time when the inmates had begun to take over the asylum.

A couple of years ago when I went out to California to attend the big auction at which MGM sold all of the props, costumes, furniture, vehicles and anything else that could bring in money, I made it a point to walk over to the star dressing room building. I looked up, and there still was the felt board. And, sure enough, Kathryn Grayson had become just an indentation. There was only one thing different about the board—there wasn't a single name in white lettering. This meant just one thing: The Hollywood star system was dead. It gave me a sad feeling that day. And it saddens me now, to write about something that was so terribly important to the movie business.

Recently I tried to find that felt board, but it has disappeared. No one seems to know whether or not it had been sold at auction. No one cares! I care! If possible, I'd like to own it, as a memento of something special that once was but is no longer.

# A Glamorous Bash—
and Elizabeth Taylor

One of the stars I have been questioned about most, over a period of years, is Elizabeth Taylor. I've met her several times, but have actually interviewed her only once.

The first time I met Elizabeth was at a party Kathryn Grayson gave for Zsa Zsa Gabor's birthday. Katie and Zsa Zsa both have birthdays in February a few days apart. At the time Zsa Zsa (my favorite Hungarian) was allegedly the same age as Kathryn. Katie, with her lovely musical laugh says now, "I happen to have the damnable habit of getting a year older each year, and some other actresses don't."

Apparently that's the truth, because in some of her interviews I've read that the beautiful Zsa Zsa (and she is truly a beauty) could be almost young enough to date David Cassidy. Just an added note about Zsa Zsa: in spite of the frivolous and vain image that comes across on those late-night talk shows, she is a loyal and good friend to those people she loves.

Back to the Grayson party, which took place in two of the private dining rooms at the Beverly Hills Hotel; cocktails in one room and dinner in another.

You can imagine how exciting that dinner was for

me. I had never before been in the company of so many really big stars. During the cocktail hour I chatted with Elizabeth and Michael Wilding. There never was a more beautiful young lady than Elizabeth Taylor. Her violet eyes were definitely hypnotic. I wish I could say the same for her conversation at that time. Michael Wilding, though, was utterly charming.

The weather had been so bad during that February with heavy rains, that there were sand bags along Sunset Boulevard to fend off sliding debris. Therefore, I couldn't understand how Mr. Wilding had a deep tan. When I asked him, he said, "Oh, the sun comes out for a little bit each day, and when it does I run out and sit beside my pool to catch some of it!" I'm sure Elizabeth Taylor Hilton Wilding Todd Fisher Burton has by now forgotten her words, but I remember them: she said, "You mean you sit beside 'our' pool!" Implying, I thought, that she had paid at least in part for that pool.

He apologized to Elizabeth, saying, "I'm sorry. I mean our pool."

I had never been with Robert Taylor socially before Kathryn's party, although I had met him on movie sets. He had been divorced for several years from Barbara Stanwyck and was going with Ursula Thiess, whom he subsequently married.

I asked Kathryn to seat me beside Bob Taylor at the dinner table. I had been crazy about him since *A Yank at Oxford* and I thought he was the handsomest man in the whole world. Katie said she couldn't do it, because single men like to sit with their girls. She could, however, split up any of the married couples without difficulties. Was there a married man I would like to sit next to?

There wasn't! So I did something pretty awful. If Katie hadn't been such a good friend she wouldn't be talking to me today. Now, so many years later, we laugh about it.

While everyone was still having drinks, I sneaked into the dining room where an enormous oblong table had been carefully set with place cards. All right, so you've guessed. I switched the place cards, making sure Ursula Thiess was still on Taylor's right but I put myself on his left.

I'll never forget the array of gorgeous people around that table. I can't remember the entire guest list, but I do recall looking around at Fernando Lamas with Arlene Dahl (he had just broken up his romance with Lana Turner), Stewart Granger with his then wife Jean Simmons, Mimi Benzell who was in L.A. to do a concert, the Wildings, Ava Gardner with Sidney Guillaroff, Jack Warner, head of Warner Brothers, with some countess wearing a dress cut to the midriff.

I managed to keep poor Robert Taylor so engaged in conversation throughout dinner he barely had a chance to talk to the lady he wanted to be with.

Even though Taylor was definitely the most beautiful man there, his conversation wasn't exactly exhilarating or romantic. But then why should it have been with me? We talked about his horses, his ranch and how he and Ursula liked to pack a picnic basket and go out somewhere near his stables to spend the day. Talking about horse manure wasn't my idea of glamour, but I didn't care. I just wanted to look at him. And for two solid hours that's exactly what I did.

Taylor may not have been a very romantic table companion but the whole evening was certainly romantic. Kathryn had strolling violinists playing throughout dinner. At some point they played songs from Lehar's *The Merry Widow*. This started Fernando Lamas singing right from his chair. (He had made *The Merry Widow* with Turner.) Then from her place at the head of the table, Kathryn joined him in a duet. Stewart Granger sang! The musicians strolled over to Mimi and played music from *Traviata* and she, too, burst into song. Pretty soon the whole table was singing in chorus. Can you imagine how exciting that was for "show-business movie-struck" me? The only jarring note of the night came from Jack Warner who toasted the birthday girl Zsa Zsa and his hostess, Kathryn. His speech was smutty and in bad taste. I was shocked to think that a head of a big business corporation (because that's what Warner Brothers is) would say some of the things he did. I had been brought up around corporation presidents, but not the likes of Jack Warner.

Sometime during the evening, I learned that this was the norm for Mr. Warner. I was told that in deference to his hostess, he was a lot more delicate than usual.

After dinner, we all went into the Persian Room where the hotel orchestra played for dancing. No, Robert Taylor did not ask me to dance. I kept hoping he would because the Persian Room was open to the public, and there were several people there I knew from back home. I'm sure Mr. Taylor had had his fill of me at the dinner table.

To get back to Elizabeth Taylor, the one real interview I had with her took place by designed accident. In 1959, Elizabeth Taylor was nominated for an Academy Award for her marvelous performance in *Cat on a Hot Tin Roof*. This nomination came around the time she and Eddie Fisher were in the throes of a torrid romance following the death of her husband, Mike Todd, in a plane accident.

On the way into the Santa Monica Civic Auditorium, where the awards were being held, the crowds outside screamed for Liz and Eddie. Their notoriety value together that year was tremendous. It was the year when Liz allegedly swiped Eddie away from her friend Debbie Reynolds. The cameramen and reporters went crazy snapping away at the couple photographically and verbally as the pair valiantly tried to get to their assigned seats.

At the conclusion of the show I watched Oscar loser Elizabeth Taylor sit very still in her seat alongside of

Mr. Fisher, as the people filed out of the auditorium paying no attention to them at all. The media—radio, television and newspaper reporters scurried after the winners. No one, besides myself, seemed interested any longer in Elizabeth Taylor.

Then I watched the pair get up and walk dejectedly out a side door. The sprint I made to get to them could have beaten the last Olympics' record-breaking hundred-yard dash. With a small tape recorder in hand, I sprang out at them. They were so stunned to discover that a member of the press was still interested, they gave me a great interview.

Eddie was angry. He felt Liz lost the Oscar because of all the unfavorable publicity they were receiving concerning their private lives. I had to agree with him that Elizabeth Taylor did certainly deserve to win. Elizabeth, whether she meant it or not, disagreed with us and said, "It was won fairly and squarely by Simone Signoret for *Room at the Top*." She then went on to tell me of her and Eddie's plans to get married, etc., etc. She spent twenty minutes talking with me, which are twenty minutes more than I've been able to get with her since.

In 1961, Elizabeth Taylor (who had become Mrs. Eddie Fisher) received an Oscar for her performance in the film *Butterfield 8*. A lot of people felt it was given to her belatedly for the one she should have won the year before.

I couldn't get to interview her in the auditorium when she won, but I managed to speak with her later for a moment during the Academy Award ball. I'm sure she didn't remember me, but she was so happy to be sitting there with the coveted Oscar in front of her that she talked to everyone who came up to the table—and I was in the "everyone" category this time.

# Will the Real
# Howard Hughes Stand Up?

So many times I am asked if I ever met Howard Hughes. No, I never met him, although I have seen him and I have spoken to him on the telephone.

A long time ago, years before he ever lived in Las Vegas, I saw Mr. Hughes in the cocktail lounge of the Desert Inn. He was not yet a recluse and people knew who he was. What did he look like? He was very tall, good-looking, had a mustache and, yes, he was wearing sneakers. No one paid special attention to him, except the usual attention a regular patron receives. Someone pointed him out, and I was intrigued enough, even then, to look over at him.

Kathryn Grayson knew Howard Hughes well. She definitely was never one of his "girls," although he had proposed to her. One always heard the rumor that Howard Hughes stashed his various girlfriends away in houses around the hills of Hollywood. Some of them, the legend goes, with their mothers. I don't know if he had proposed marriage to any of these gals, but you can bet those with live-in mothers expected him to marry them. If they didn't, their mothers did!

Kathryn was very young, very beautiful, a very successful movie star and extremely independent. She wanted nothing from Mr. Hughes except his friendship, which she had. She truly liked him as a human being. Howard saw Katie, but they never went out on dates. He always came to visit her at her palatial Santa Monica estate. He also was very fond of her baby daughter Patti-Kate (who is now a young married lady).

I lived in New York at the time and over the long-distance phone I'd tell Katie, if she happened to mention that "H.H." had come a-visiting, "Marry him, for God's sake!" I could think of nothing more exciting than to be married to the richest, most sought after man in the world. If it couldn't happen to me, then second best was to be the friend of the girl who was married to the richest, most sought after man in the world!

Although she might not admit it now, she found Howard's courtship exciting. He would come visiting at any hour of the day or night. His henchmen would telephone ahead to say that he was on his way. Of course, she wasn't always in when they called, and then he'd leave a name, any name except his own. But, she always knew who it was.

In those days I made only one trip a year to L.A., usually around Academy-Award time. One year, I remember that Katie picked me up at the airport and we drove back to the Beverly Hills Hotel. We had dinner in the hotel's dining room, after which we went upstairs to my room where we sat talking and gossiping.

About 10:30 P.M., Kathryn went home. Her house in Santa Monica is about a twenty-minute drive from the Beverly Hills Hotel. Almost as soon as she left, the phone rang and a high-pitched nasal male voice asked, "Is Miss Grayson still there?" I explained that she had just left and, in case she called me later, I asked him who was calling so I could tell her.

The high-pitched voice on the other end of the

phone replied, "Norman Taurog." (Norman Taurog was [and is] a very famous Hollywood director.) He politely thanked me and said he would call her at home.

About an hour later Katie called and said, "Well— you spoke to the *man*." I assumed she meant Mr. Taurog and said so. "No, silly," she said. "That was Howard, Howard Hughes. For some reason he checks up on my comings and goings, and he told me he called your room at the hotel and that he had spoken to my friend Shirley Eder Slotkin."

Wow, that was spooky considering the fact that Katie never once mentioned my name to him. For a guy who was not betrothed or going steady with Kathryn, or even going out on real dates with her, it was strange that he kept such tabs on her. Maybe he kept tabs on everyone he knew.

W-e-l-l, *I* spoke to Howard Hughes! How many people can say that? Recently, during the Clifford Irving hoopla, I listened on television to his denial of the Irving story. The voice allegedly belonged to Hughes, and I tried hard to recognize that voice, which was silly on my part since I had heard it only once in my life, some twenty years earlier. If I had been put under oath to do so, I could never have identified that voice coming over the air.

During the era of Hughes's courtship of Kathryn Grayson her house was always filled with masses of flowers. Many times, nestled somewhere in those flowers were exquisite jewels. Katie, coming from that old school of "I may accept only books, candy and flowers from a man," kept the flowers and returned the gems. When she told me about some of the things she found in the flowers, I'd say, "You are absolutely right! A lady never accepts jewelry from a man unless she is engaged to him." That's how young and dumb we both were. Today, I'm a whole lot wiser. If I were told the same thing now, I'd say "Send back the flowers and keep the baubles." I don't know if Kathryn would keep the jewels today, even if she is a friend of Zsa Zsa Gabor's.

For years and years, Howard Hughes kept several bungalows he never used at the Beverly Hills Hotel. Recently the night doorman Ron Jones, who is also in the Cadillac rental business, told me a fascinating Hughes story.

Back in 1959, someone in the Hughes office called to rent a special sedan. So Ron went out and bought a new Cadillac with all of Hughes's specifications. He paid $5,500 for it, then rented it to Hughes at the going rate—$125 a week.

That car made one trip to the Los Angeles International Airport and back to the hotel. That was it! After the trip it was parked outside on the street for two full years, and Hughes paid $24,000 in rental fees. After two years the car was turned back to Ron, who in turn sold it for $3,500.

Ron never stopped grinning the whole while he was telling me this story. It makes you wonder how many other people benefited from Howard Hughes's eccentricities.

But it was such eccentricities, I'm sure, that decided Kathryn Grayson against accepting his proposal of marriage. Suppose she had accepted? Would he have gone through with a wedding? Well, that's something we won't know unless H.H. decides to write his own book.

# My First Ocean Voyage

On a Saturday afternoon, years ago, I went to an auction of paintings at the Park-Bernet Galleries in New York with Kathleen Winsor whose novel *Forever Amber* at the time was the number-one book on all best-seller lists. On the way out we bumped into a friend of mine who, in the course of conversation, said that her husband was coming in from England two days later on the *Queen Mary*. And that perhaps after he got back we could get together for dinner.

When I returned to our Washington Square apartment, I found a cable from Kathryn Grayson that said she and her husband, Johnny Johnston, would be arriving in two days on the *Queen Mary*, and for Edward and me to plan on having dinner with them that night at the Plaza Hotel.

A better and more exciting plan popped into my head. I would meet them out at sea! With a little pull and a press pass I managed to get on board the Coast Guard cutter which met the ocean liners out at quarantine where they had to stop before docking in New York. I was told it took a couple of hours from the time the Coast Guard boarded a ship until she slowly chugged into "her berth" on the Hudson River.

At 5:30 A.M. on a windy and cold day, we went out to sea on a teeny boat to meet that enormous giant the *Queen Mary*. You have no idea how insignificant you feel as you approach that gargantuan floating vehicle. Just standing still, she made large waves which not too gently rocked our little boat.

There she was, waiting for us as we pulled up alongside her. This was my first experience of climbing from a tender onto an ocean liner, and it was really scary. I was wearing a hat with a big tall feather, and my biggest concern was how I was going to hold onto my hat with one hand and climb a rope ladder holding on with the other.

Of course we didn't have to climb a rope ladder. A gangplank from the bowels of the ship was set up and we walked easily aboard that big "mother."

It seemed as if all the passengers were leaning over the rail watching us come aboard. I looked up, and sure enough, there were Johnny and Kathryn wildly screaming to me. Kathryn kept shouting, "I don't believe it! I really don't believe it!"

Once aboard Her Majesty's ship, the Coast Guard immediately went about its chores of checking passports in the grand salon. And the press went about its business of catching up with the varied social, theatrical and political celebrities coming in from Europe.

After lots of kissing and hugging with Johnny and Katie, I tipped a steward to set up one deck chair just for me. You see, at this final point of a sea voyage, the chairs are stowed, and all the decks are cleared for arrival in port. Since this was my first voyage on an ocean liner (about one hour's worth), I was going to do it in style. In the movies people were always wrapped up in blankets in deck chairs, and I wanted to see how it would feel.

There were many people I knew on board. Some stopped scurrying about doing their last-minute tipping and packing to chat as they saw me. All of them

asked, "What are you doing here? How come this is
the first time we've seen you during the trip?"

My reply was simply, "I never come out of my
stateroom until the last few hours of a sea voyage!"

Among the people who saw me in the chair was the
husband of the girl I had met two days before at the
Parke-Bernet Galleries.

After the tugs, at snail-like pace, docked the *Queen
Mary,* I walked down the gangplank in front of Katie
and Johnny *and* directly behind the husband of "that
girl," waving, just like everybody else, to those waiting
on the dock for the arrival of loved ones.

My friend from Parke-Bernet was standing there
waiting for her husband to set foot on terra firma. He
put his arms out to embrace her, but she was so
stunned seeing me come down that gangplank, she
never went into his waiting arms. Instead she came
up to me and said, "Shirley, how could you possibly
be arriving from Europe? Didn't I see you two days
ago with Kathleen Winsor at the Parke-Bernet Galleries?"

Discovering a mean streak I never knew I had till
then, I replied, "Who, me? You couldn't have seen
me. I just came in from London."

I stood with Kathryn and Johnny under the letter
"J" as they waited for the customs officials to go
through their luggage. Minutes later, my friend from
Parke-Bernet ran over to where we were and asked
again "Shirley, didn't we, two days ago, talk about
having dinner one night?"

I looked at her as if she were out of her mind,
which, indeed, she appeared to be at that moment.

I turned around to Kathryn Grayson, whom I had
clued in on this horrendous practical joke, saying,
"Katie, will you please tell 'so-and-so' where we have
all just come from."

White-lied Kathryn, "You boarded the *Queen Mary*
five days ago with us in London."

That evening my victim called saying, "I'm going

out of my mind. I haven't even properly greeted my husband because of you. He says he saw you sitting in a steamer chair wrapped up in a blanket this morning. How is that possible?"

Not really wanting to see her taken off to Bellevue in a strait jacket, I told her the truth. She slammed down the phone and from that day to this has never talked to me again. Well, we had never been close friends anyway! Thinking back on it, though, I can't blame her.

These are the rotten things you do when you are very young. I wonder if I could do it all over again today? Yep, I think I could, except for one change. Today I wouldn't go out to sea to meet *any* friend at 5:30 A.M.

# My Most Ashamed Moment

Maybe it's macabre to admit to having a wonderful time at a funeral, but, so help me, I enjoyed myself at one which took place in Hollywood in the 1950s.

I had a date to meet Kathryn Grayson in the famed MGM commissary for lunch. That morning she called in tears, saying, "Shirley, one of my dearest friends at MGM, Ida Koverman, died and the funeral is today." She went on to explain that Ida Koverman had been Louis B. Mayer's executive secretary, and before that had been President Herbert Hoover's executive secretary.

"She was like a mother to so many of us," continued Katie. "A whole group of MGM alumni are meeting at the commissary for lunch, and we are going on to the funeral as a group. I'm sure you wouldn't enjoy eating there today."

You feel badly when you hear anyone has passed on, but since I didn't know the lady who died, I naturally wasn't that upset. I told Katie I would meet her anyway for lunch, and then go on my own way when they took off for the funeral.

Well, there I was, seated at a table with Van Johnson, Clark Gable, Greer Garson and so many other big Metro names. They were all reminiscing about Miss Koverman. Apparently she had done something nice for each and every one of them. She seemed truly loved.

Not being in a hurry to leave such an illustrious group of stars, I decided to go along with them to the funeral. I remember riding in the limousine to the Pierce Funeral Chapel with Van, Katie and several others. When we arrived, the street was filled with people; movie fans, reporters, photographers and even TV cameras were located in strategic spots to catch the expected stars.

The familiar faces all wore dark glasses to hide their tears as they filed in for a last view of the body. I hadn't exactly planned to go inside, but somehow I was pushed into the chapel by the momentum of the crowd, sandwiched in between Robert Taylor and June Allyson.

There I was, unexpectedly on my way to view the body of a woman I had never seen in life. Actually, I never saw her in death either, because by being pushed straight on by the crowd, I managed to keep my eyes tightly shut all the way. The chapel was so overcrowded, many mourners, including the group I came with, filed right back out onto the street where the services could be heard over a loud speaker.

I didn't know Barbara Stanwyck then, nor had I ever seen her in person before. There I was standing next to her as she attentively listened to the service. Everyone stood out on that street with his head bowed except me. I kept looking around, making mental notes of who was there, not totally unaware of the whirring of the television cameras.

Later that evening on the six and eleven o'clock news, I made my West Coast TV debut. Because it was so difficult for the cameramen to catch the stars with their dark glasses and their heads bowed, their cameras sometimes focused on glassesless me.

The phone never stopped ringing that night, with

people calling to say, "Hey, did you see yourself on television?" And, "Boy, you sure were in good company!" I'm ashamed to admit that I did have a fine time just mingling!

Kathryn has since told me so many wonderful things about the late Ida Koverman, I feel more and more ashamed of having enjoyed myself that day. Katie also has reminded me that I kept mumbling during the service about Stanwyck: "She's got such a young face, why did she let her hair go gray? She's too young to wear gray hair!"

Also, since the day of her funeral, I've learned that it was Ida Koverman who was responsible for MGM's hiring of Robert Taylor and Clark Gable. Mr. Mayer did not want to put them under contract, and it was through her efforts that they were signed. Louis B. Mayer, happily for MGM, more often than not heeded her advice. Miss Koverman, too, was a buffer between the stars and Mayer. If he was displeased with any one of them, I'm told it was she who soothed the boss, thereby helping the star to avoid his terrible temper. No wonder Ida Koverman was so beloved by all those stars who worked with her.

# Joan Crawford Makes Points for New Girl in Town

When we moved to Detroit from New York, I was a stringer reporter for NBC "Monitor," but because I had no local media affiliation, I wasn't invited to very many press luncheons, dinners or conferences. When I did manage to wangle an invite, I was completely ignored by my "established" peers. Oh, they were polite enough, because people in Detroit are generally polite. But I was looked on as an interloper, if I was looked at (or on) at all.

Then one day Joan Crawford came to town to plug her latest movie *Queen Bee*, and, thanks to her, the other reporters changed their attitude toward me.

I had met Joan while she was filming *Sudden Fear* in Hollywood. The producer of the movie, Joseph Kaufman (now deceased), was a close family friend who allowed me to come and go from the Crawford set.

You can imagine how surprised I was to receive a phone call from the local press agent in charge of arranging the press luncheon in Miss Crawford's honor at the Sheraton Cadillac Hotel.

I can remember part of the conversation as if it were yesterday. He said, "Miss Eder, we have been advised by a spokesman for Miss Joan Crawford that we are to make sure you are invited to her press luncheon. Obviously, you are a close personal friend of hers."

Well, I wouldn't exactly call our relationship, at that point, close or personal. I didn't realize she even knew I was living in Detroit—when we met, we were still living in New York.

I have, however, since learned that Miss Crawford knows everything necessary about anyone she has ever met. She has a terrific memory for names. When she sees someone she has met possibly just once, she not only calls him or her by name but also inquires about members of their families.

The luncheon for Miss Crawford was called for noon I walked around the room trying hard to mingle. As I said, the others were polite, but that was it! Miss Crawford did not come down from her suite for forty-five minutes. Anticipation kept mounting, and all the conversations during those forty-five minutes concerned the star—the lady knew what she was doing by arriving late.

Then she made her entrance!

She strode briskly into the room followed by an entourage of people.

Miss Crawford was dramatically dressed. By golly, when she came in, you knew someone "special" had arrived. She's a movie star who always looks exactly as you expect a movie star to look.

She apologized for being late, then she walked about the room shaking hands and addressing people by names. And each one was flattered to be remembered.

I planned to wait patiently in a corner until after she had greeted all the others, then go up and say, "Hi, I'm Shirley Eder. I met you with Joe Kaufman when you were making *Sudden Fear.*"

It didn't happen that way. Miss Crawford said, looking around the room, "Is Shirley Eder here?"

From my private corner I answered, "I'm here." She came right over and kissed me on the cheek.

Now everyone turned in our direction to see who Shirley Eder was. She said aloud, "Hello, darling, it's so nice to see you again. I bring love to you from——" and she named several mutual friends in Los Angeles and New York.

Then it was time to go into the other room for lunch, where there was a large horseshoe-shaped table with Miss Crawford seated directly in the center. As for the rest of us, your rank in town determined where you sat. The movie critics and top radio and TV people sat closest to her. I was placed far down at the end of one side of the table. (At least I was closest to the ladies' room.)

Just as we all sat down, Miss Crawford turned to the person on her left and said, "Would you mind changing places with Shirley Eder? We are old friends and we have so much to talk about. You see, we don't get to see each other often. I'm sure you understand."

In a matter of moments I was moved to the center of the table on Miss Crawford's left.

Well, there I was sitting next to "J.C." What's more, we found ourselves talking together as if we really were old friends.

I don't think Joan Crawford knows to this day, how she upped my prestige in Detroit.

Right after the dessert (which Miss Crawford did not even taste) the press conference started. No baseball player ever fielded balls better than Miss Crawford fielded questions. She answered those she wanted to; the rest, she chose to ignore.

I watched this fabulously professional woman adeptly turn what might have been a disaster (for someone else) into a delightful performance.

A lady critic on one of the Detroit newspapers had three or six too many martinis. Sitting close to Miss Crawford, in slurring speech she said, "Say, Joan, I saw a preview of *Queen Bee* yesterday. What a stinker it is. How did you get euchred into making that one?"

Just as if she were doing a sleight of hand trick, Miss Crawford jumped up from her seat and announced, "You've all read about the reversible mink coat I wear in the film. It is one color mink on the inside and another color on the outside, and I can wear it inside out if I choose. I have it here with me. Would you all like to see it?"

Since the luncheon guests were predominantly female, they called out in unison, "Yes, yes, let's see it!"

Joan said, "I'll be back in just a few minutes. Why don't you all have some more dessert?" With that she floated out of the room followed by her secretary, wardrobe lady, security guard and public relations man. Joan deserved a standing ovation for her ability to turn a bad situation to her advantage.

Twenty minutes later she came back wearing the mink coat, first on one side, then on the other. There were audible "oohs" and "aahs" from all of us.

When the conference ended, Joan invited me to the Presidential Suite (she always has a Presidential Suite) for a more personal visit. By now I had begun to feel we had always been best friends.

Once upstairs, Joan Crawford very businesslike, said "All right, Shirley, how important is so-and-so (the sloshed critic) in this town? How much weight does she carry with the readers? What is the name of her editor? Her publisher?"

I couldn't answer all her questions since I was so new to Detroit, but I told her that I had heard that same lady critic was actually a big Joan Crawford fan.

"Oh," exclaimed Joan in a much gentler tone. That obviously changed Joan's fighting tactics. If I had visions of Miss Crawford having the lady fired, I was all wrong.

Some ten days later I met the critic at another press luncheon (I was being invited to all of them now). When she saw me, she proudly opened her purse, took out a letter and read it to me. It was a beautiful personal letter from Joan Crawford. I wasn't singled out by the critic to hear the contents of the letter, but she proudly showed it to everyone else there. From that day until the critic's death several years later, Joan Crawford could do no wrong, on or off screen.

Incidentally, the critic's review of Joan Crawford and her *Queen Bee* was honest but not offensive. She gave it more praise than it deserved.

J.C., now that we have become good friends, this chapter is written as a belated "thank you" note for helping to set me up as a "real" reporter in Motor City.

# Ginger Rogers

Ginger Rogers came to Detroit to try out a Broadway musical comedy, *Pink Jungle*. It was produced by Paul Gregory, who is now married to Janet Gaynor. Another star in *Pink Jungle* was Agnes Moorehead. It was through Agnes, whom I knew, that I was able to watch rehearsals.

Sitting in the back of the orchestra during those rehearsals I got to know a vitally alive, intelligent lady, Lela Rogers, Ginger's mother. And, eventually, Lela set up an interview for me with her daughter in their suite at the Sheraton Cadillac Hotel.

I was certainly a Ginger Rogers fan—who isn't? I suppose I expected her to be somewhat formidable because she was such a superstar. Instead I discovered a charming lady with disarming warmth. Even though she was plenty tired from a long day's rehearsal, she answered most of my questions. Those she didn't want to answer, she pleasantly, and politely said, "No comment."

Most mothers are proud of their children and Lela Rogers is no exception, but perhaps she is a little more honest.

Right in front of me, she gave Ginger motherly and

professional advice. "Ginger," she said, "there are many things which should be cut out of this show—including a couple of your songs. Your singing voice has never been *that* good!"

Ginger laughed and said, "It's tough to take that from your own mother."

At the end of the interview, Ginger Rogers asked, "Shirley, will you come back to see me after the opening? I'd like your honest opinion of the show." You can imagine how flattering that was, even though I suspected at the time she didn't really mean it.

A couple of nights later we went to the opening of *Pink Jungle* and I did go backstage, but certainly not to give my opinion because I hated the show. I was going back just to say, "Hi," and dash out.

The hall outside the dressing room was jammed with people, including top executives from Ford and General Motors, and lots of celebs who had flown in from New York and Hollywood. I stood in line with all of them waiting to make it into the star's dressing room. By the time I got in, other people were still there, including Henry Ford II. I waved to Ginger, in the midst of all the excitement, and mumbled something like "You were just fine," then turned to leave. Ginger lunged forward and grabbed me by the wrist saying, "Please don't go, I'd like you to wait and talk with me."

What a terrible spot to be in. She obviously really did want my opinion of the show. I didn't know her well enough to say it was just plain lousy and in my opinion should not go on to Broadway. As she was saying good-by to her visitors, I used the time to mentally invent tactful untruths. How could a Shirley Eder, newly come to Detroit, tell "the" Ginger Rogers the plain and simple truth? I was not yet a columnist: I merely had a radio show in Detroit and did interviews for NBC's "Monitor."

Ginger's last well wisher departed, and now came the moment of truth (or untruth). Only the two of us were left in the flower-filled dressing room. With her blue, blue eyes, she looked me square in my nondescript ones and said, "Well, tell me the truth. What did you think of it?" Her honesty forced me to blurt out, "*Pink Jungle* should change its title to *Pink Eye*. It's awful!" What was I saying? "I knew I could count on you for the truth," answered Ginger. I don't know how she knew, since I had definitely not planned to tell it like it was. I'm not a believer in astrology nor is she, but maybe both of us, being born under the sign of the crab (she on July 16, me on July 11) had something to do with it.

Matter of fact, as the years went by and we became close friends, sometimes just as I was thinking about her, she would call from California. I mean at that very second. Many times over the years, when I've called her she'd say, "I just had my hand on the phone to dial you."

Ginger went on to several other cities with *Pink Jungle,* but absolutely refused to go into New York with it. Because she wouldn't continue in it, Paul Gregory brought her up on charges before Equity (the actors' union). Arbitration between them went on for several years. I still don't know who won, but I think everybody connected with *Pink Jungle* was a winner, simply because it never opened on Broadway.

When I first met Ginger, she was recently divorced from Jacques Bergerac. Before Jacques, she had been married to Jack Culpepper, to Lew Ayres and to Jack Briggs. Ginger Rogers, a devout Christian Scientist, doesn't smoke or drink or even cuss. Despite the four marriages (up to then), she was pretty trusting when it came to men. Like many other female stars, she was susceptible to flattery from tall good-looking virile guys who devoted their time and energy to catering to susceptible ladies.

I can hear her now saying, "Shirley, if you see me falling for that kind of man again, tell me. I trust you and I'd like you to tell me the truth." Did you ever try to tell a woman that the guy she is crazy about is all wrong for her? Don't bother, she won't listen.

Twice, in the ensuing years, not in words, but in actions, I attempted to dissuade Ginger from falling for two men. One near mistake she spotted herself (but another glamorous star didn't and has since divorced him), and the other she married, in spite of the whisperings among her friends of "he's so wrong for *her*." Unfortunately, nobody bothered to tell Ginger assuming that a woman in love would pay little or no attention, anyway. Only recently, she divorced husband number five, William Marshall. I didn't know Ginger Rogers during her other marriages, but I watched her try very hard to make this one work.

From the beginning of our friendship, I realized, although I think Ginger to this day is unaware of the fact, that she is attracted to men who excel in tennis, golf and swimming. She is an aficionado of the outdoor life.

Can you imagine the excitement in our house the first time Ginger Rogers came to stay with us? My husband remembers it well because the entire household was in constant upheaval. I visited her house in Beverly Hills and knew that she liked to sit down at a dressing table while making up. We had no dressing table in the guest room, but you can bet by the time she arrived with her housekeeper, confidante and friend of more than thirty years, Irma Scheid, there was a brand-new dressing table and chair in that guest room. Would you believe she never once used it, preferring to stand up in front of the bathroom mirror to apply her eye makeup and lipstick. When she wasn't performing or appearing in public, that was the only makeup Ginger Rogers wore.

Miss Rogers is also a fresh-air nut. While she was at our house, we learned that hot or cold, when she went to sleep at night she not only opened the windows wide, but slept at the foot of the bed, instead of at the head as does everyone else. She also kept her door open so that the air could properly circulate around her. I thought about chaining my husband to our bed while she was in residence because the guest-room door was wide open all night.

Also, I slept with my eyes wide open in case my husband decided to sleep walk! Ginger loved Edward and still does, and he adores her. As a matter of fact, her pet name for him is "Twinkie," a derivative of "Twinkle Toes" and thereby hangs this tale!

After Ginger left *Pink Jungle* she went to New York to stay where you would expect a big movie star to stay—at the Waldorf Towers. In the three weeks we had become friends, prior to her departure from Detroit, she often said, "I wish I could meet a fine upstanding decent businessman. Somehow, that kind of man never calls me." The reason, as my husband explained to her many years later, was because an honest-to-goodness businessman wouldn't have the guts to call Ginger Rogers for a date.

Well, we were going into New York to spend the Christmas holidays with my parents, and I was determined to introduce Ginger to a businessman. I asked her if it was all right if we invited a very tall, distinguished, handsome automotive executive to go out with us as a foursome in New York. She was delighted.

When I called the auto executive about the date he said, "You've got to be kidding! Ginger Rogers wouldn't go out with me." It took some convincing to persuade him that she really would.

Came the night of the big double date in New York. In a rented limousine we picked up Ginger's date at the Yale Club, where he had apparently fortified himself with enough booze to give him the courage to face the evening ahead. Over and over again he repeated, "What am I doing here?" When we arrived in front of the Waldorf Towers, he jumped out of the back of the car and promptly bounced into the front seat next to the driver, telling my husband,

"Edward, you go get her." In less than nothing flat, Edward sprinted from the limo past the doorman into the hotel. I never knew before that he could run so fast!

From the front seat, Mr. X turned and made conversation with me, about anything and everything except the evening ahead.

Some ten minutes later, out came Ginger Rogers, looking divine in a short red dress which swirled about her knees as she walked. She was on the arm of my husband whose expression said, "Look at me—I am a combination of Cary Grant, Clark Gable and Fred Astaire." Mr. X got out of the car, shook hands with his date, then, so help me, got back into the front seat. Edward sat with his girls—me and the Other one.

We went to El Morocco for dinner. The music was inviting, I was dying to dance, but Edward couldn't ask me to because each time he mumbled something about the music, Mr. X kicked him under the table. If we danced that meant he would then have to ask Ginger. He kept drinking and talking to me which, of course, left Ginger all to my husband. After dessert, Mr. X having summoned the courage at last to speak to her, said, "Say, tell me, Ginger, how can you, having been in the business such a long time and so successfully, have picked a turkey like *Pink Jungle?*" That was just for openers!

"Mr. X," replied Ginger Rogers calling him "Mr." instead of by his first name, "suppose you tell me, how you and the other automotive executives, having been so successful for so many years, choose to make cars that come off the assembly lines—lemons? You see, Mr. X, on the drawing board your cars, designed by the top men in their field and executed by so-called automotive geniuses, look great, don't they? Then how come, by the time they are ready for the road, they don't come out as they were planned, and the public rejects them? You see," she patiently explained, "it's the same in show business."

"Hey," exclaimed her date, "that's a good one. I must remember to tell it at our next meeting." Now was the time for all good men to come to her rescue, so my husband, a very good man, took Ginger by the hand and said, "Let's dance." And did they ever dance, and dance and dance! A grin from ear to ear stayed on his face as he executed steps of the fox trot, waltz and even the rhumba (which he never would do with me). At any moment I expected him to leap across the tables with Ginger in his arms, à la Fred Astaire.

Finally Mr. X turned to me and asked, "Wanna dance?" I got up on the floor to dance and to keep an eye on you know who.

"Why," I asked my partner, "didn't you ask your own date to dance? It was the polite thing to do."

"Aw," replied this six foot-five handsome hulk of a man, "I wouldn't know how to dance with Ginger Rogers."

Hours later, when we got back into the car, Mr. X still up front with the chauffeur, Ginger looked up into my Edward's eyes and said, "From now on and forever more I shall call you 'Twinkie'—short for Twinkle Toes." And that's exactly what she has called him from that day to this.

Mr. X, also, from that day to this, refers to Edward as Twinkle Toes. You can bet Ginger Rogers doesn't even recall Mr. X, but assuredly he has never forgotten his date with Ginger Rogers.

# Tennis Anyone?

Ginger Rogers is heralded as a fine tennis player. After having known her just a short time, it was exciting to be invited to her house to play on her court, because over the years I had read about all the famous people who had played there.

In the middle of winter, soon after Ginger's invitation, Edward and I planned a vacation trip to Los Angeles. After fifteen years of not having played tennis, I decided to do something to remedy the situation before we left.

At that time there were no indoor courts around Detroit—tennis in Motor City was definitely *out* in the winter. But I was damned if I'd look inept and foolish when the time came to play tennis with Ginger Rogers. Sooooo I went over to the Hamtramck High School where its principal, Jean Hoxie (now deceased), was considered one of the top teaching pros in the country.

I hadn't realized that she trained her kids in the gymnasium by having them hit the ball against the wall and to each other—without a net! Jean had me join a class comprised of children from ages seven to seventeen. Matter of fact, it was one of her pupils, about nine years old, who showed me how to hit the ball against the wall. The name of that little kid was "Peaches" Bartkowicz. Peaches has since become one of the ranking female tennis players in America. (I have not!)

Mrs. Hoxie fitted me with a racket that seemed to weigh a ton simply because it had been so long since I had even held one. Also, she had those little monsters run me ragged all over that gym. After the second visit I pulled a couple of long unused leg ligaments and had to walk on crutches for several weeks.

Mrs. Hoxie knew why I wanted to relearn tennis. And since she was a devout Ginger Rogers fan, she insisted I continue, if only to hit the ball against the wall while leaning on one crutch.

The kids in the school loved to watch the old lady (me) hitting balls, sometimes with the crutch instead of with the racket.

Tennis, in 1960, was still not "in," and it was impossible at that time of the year to buy a proper tennis outfit anywhere in Michigan.

Off the crutches and now with a cane, I flew to Bergdorf Goodman's in New York to look for a tennis dress chic enough to wear on a movie star's court. I found one which had an emblem of crossed tennis rackets on its pocket. I also bought white tennis shorts and a white polo shirt (with matching crossed tennis rackets on it) for my husband. He hadn't played the game in over twenty years. He had no time, though, to work out with Mrs. Hoxie. And I bought two pairs of brand-new Bergdorf sneakers—one pair for me and the other for my daughter.

Off to California we went in a blaze of crossed tennis rackets. Then the time came to put up or shut up! Arriving at 11 A.M. California time, I called Ginger and said, "We're here. When do we play?"

"Right now," she answered. "We've got a game going already. I'll pop down to the hotel to pick you up."

Ginger lived on a mountaintop near the Beverly Hills Hotel.

Well, we stood out in front looking spanking clean in our brand-new "Mr. Clean" white outfits. I held my new sneakers in hand, not wanting to get them dirty until they set foot on the court. Ginger arrived in a Cadillac convertible with the top down, seated (naturally) next to a handsome young man. (I can't remember his name because I never saw him again.)

She jumped out of the car and gave us welcoming bear hugs. Would you believe she was wearing a tiny pair of short, short shorts on her famous derrière? These shorts obviously had been used for years, they were that well worn. On top she wore a little angora bra made for her several years before by her loyal housekeeper and long-time friend, Mrs. Irma Scheid. Glancing down at the famous dancing feet, I saw a grubby old pair of sneakers. Did we ever feel foolish all slicked up in our untouched whites! What's more, there wasn't one single emblem of crossed tennis rackets on anything she wore.

Up the mountain we drove. We didn't stop at the main house, but went directly up the stairs on the lawn of her eight-acre estate, past the pool to the tennis house (also used for overnight guests).

Pointing to one of the dressing rooms she said, "You can put your shoes on in there, Shirley. Edward," she said "you come out and volley with us." I started to put my sneakers on and discovered (so help me this is the truth) that I had brought with me two right shoes! It dawned on me that my daughter's shoes and mine had gotten mixed up. So there I was with her right shoe—and my right shoe! Can you imagine how humiliating it was for me to have to go out to the court and say, "I can't play," and then have to hold up the two right shoes?

Everyone thought it was hysterically funny. Ginger said, "I'll get you a pair of mine." Did you ever wear a size 5B on a size 8AAA foot? I did that day! I can still feel the pain in my crunched-up ten toes as I limped out on the court.

Already out there volleying were my husband, John Ireland, Laurence Harvey and Ginger's date. My husband, who really was hitting the ball as well as any of them, gallantly got off the court to let me take his place. Actually, I think he was happy to just sit down. The other three men decided to stop for some iced tea.

So there we were. Ginger Rogers on one side of the net and me on the other. This was the first time I had been an any side of a net for fifteen years.

"I'll hit you a few easy ones, Shirley," called Ginger, "just so you can warm up." She hit one ball. I missed it. She hit a second ball. I missed that one too. Then she hit a third high ball which I jumped up to get. I not only missed the ball, I also ripped a ligament. Three guys carried me off the court, my husband, Laurence Harvey and John Ireland. Ginger rushed off the court too, to help rub my leg.

Nothing helped. I told them I was all right and insisted they continue playing. I wanted them all to get away from me so I could cry from the pain and the shame. (One doesn't cry in front of movie stars.) So I sat on the bench, with my leg stretched out, watching my husband competing out there with the biggies. He was good!

But as I watched him play, I also saw something extraordinary happening. His white shirt with the crossed tennis rackets was turning a deep purple. The more he perspired, the purpler his shirt became. I couldn't believe my eyes, nor could I believe this entire day.

Not being able to keep quiet any longer, I cried out: "Edward, what are you doing? You're turning purple!" All the players looked at me—then at Edward. He looked down at his shirt and thought he must have some terrible disease. Naturally, the game stopped so that everyone could examine this amazing phenomenon.

After returning the shirt to the store in New York, we learned that Edward's body chemistry was responsible for bringing out a peculiar dye in the shirt, which, according to the store manager, had never happened before.

I wonder if Ginger Rogers ever thought of selling that story to *Reader's Digest* for their section called "My Most Unforgettable Character." At least we (Edward, at any rate) were colorful.

# The Merm

We all were in the rose-decorated Standard City Club in Detroit sitting at a table with Henry Ford II and his then wife Anne, the Max Fishers and other assorted friends—the men in dinner jackets, the women in evening gowns, listening to the fabulous Ethel Merman belting out "Everything's Coming Up Roses." My husband and I were hosting a supper dance honoring Ethel after she opened in *Gypsy* in Detroit.

Way back when I was in my early teens it was Ethel Merman, during a matinee of the show called *Take a Chance*, who started my love affair with show business.

One of my schoolmates at Friends Seminary in New York was Natalie Sobol whose father, Louis Sobol, was one of the best and most loved Hollywood and Broadway columnists. His column "The Voice of Broadway" appeared six days a week in the New York *Journal-American*.

Mr. Sobol got passes to all the shows. One day Natalie invited me and a girl named Claire Schwartz to a matinee of *Take a Chance*—the show in which Ethel Merman stopped every performance cold with her singing of "Eadie Was a Lady."

Natalie couldn't care less about show business, and Claire Schwartz cared for it only moderately. But I sat in a trancelike state throughout the performance. In my imagination, I was playing each and every role up on the stage.

Mr. Sobol had given me a note to hand to Ethel Merman after the performance. That was to be my very first time backstage at a New York theatre.

But Claire Schwartz's grandmother was waiting outside the theatre to take us home, and she didn't cotton to our going backstage. Claire and Natalie didn't care one way or the other, but I was determined to meet Ethel Merman. After all, hadn't Mr. Sobol given me a note to deliver to her? That note was going to be delivered at any cost, in spite of the fact that it was now terribly crushed from having been held so tightly for two and a half hours in my hot little hand.

I remember Claire's grandmother saying, "It's getting dark and I think we should be on our way home." Somehow I managed to talk them all into walking down the alley to the stage door.

Once there I handed the note to the old stage doorman. Yep, he was exactly like all those old stage doormen we see in the movies. You know something? They still look now exactly as they did then. Maybe stage doormen live forever?

Anyway, we stood just inside the stage door watching the actors, one by one leaving the theatre. The wait for Ethel Merman seemed forever. To this day I can hear Claire's grandmother saying, "In just five minutes you are all going home! I feel foolish standing here like this. Obviously she is not going to come out."

Then just before the five minutes were up, she came out, saying, "Which one of you is Shirley Eder?"

The other two pushed me forward. In a very small voice (small, at least next to her booming one), I said, "That's me!"

I can still see and hear Ethel reading the note aloud: "Shirley Eder is a stage-struck young lady who is a friend of my daughter Natalie. They are class-mates at the same school. Ethel, introduce her to the other stars in the cast—June Knight, Jack Haley, Mitzi Mayfair and Sid Silvers. Give her a kiss which I shall return to you when I see you."

To my utter embarrassment Claire Schwartz's grandmother spoke up and said, "I told them not to bother you, Miss Merman. I told them I thought it was silly standing here like this."

How could she do that to her own granddaughter? More important, how could she so humiliate me?

Miss Merman, ignoring the grandmother's remarks, said, "Sorry, kid, but the others have already left." She signed our programs, patted me on the cheek and walked out the stage door. That pat on the cheek did it! I was hooked!

As often as possible after that, I would run up to Broadway in time to catch the curtain calls at *Take a Chance* and the exit music.

After Ethel Merman opened in *Anything Goes* at the Alvin Theatre, I made sure those Saturday lunch-eon and movie dates with my girl friends happened somewhere near the vicinity of the Alvin so I could get there in time to catch Merman's bows. If I got there early enough, the doorman out front would sometimes let me in to see the last few minutes of the show.

After a while I began to lose friends—it seems I was the only stage-struck teen-ager in the group.

Sometimes on Saturday afternoons, I stood in the alley near the stage door (it isn't that safe to stand in alleys today) watching Ethel Merman come out. She never remembered me. And of course, I never dared speak to her.

I laugh now as I remember an incident which was not funny to me at the time.

Through a friend named Thelma Savada I met two sisters, Flossie and Ruthie Yacknin. Their father was a friend of a New York stockbroker who was then squiring Ethel Merman around town. According to the gossip columns, he was her steady beau.

The Yacknin girls didn't go to Friends Seminary: I didn't really know them. How well I remember Thelma calling me one Saturday morning to say that the Yacknins were going to the matinee of *Anything Goes* and would probably have dinner with Ethel Merman. She said if I was in the alley that day she had gotten them to promise to reintroduce me to Miss Merman.

Was I ever in the alley that day! The snow was coming down and it was cold, but it didn't matter. I was happy because my friend's friends would say "hello" to me and they would be with Ethel Merman.

At last, exiting the stage door, was Ethel Merman. She had Flossie Yacknin on one arm and Ruthie Yacknin on the other. The girls were supposed to stop when they saw me and say, "Ethel, this is our friend, Shirley Eder." That's what Thelma promised they would do.

Do you know what actually did happen? Well, Flossie and Ruthie Yacknin with Ethel Merman walked right by without saying a single word to me. They didn't even bother to look to see if I was there. Do you know how devastating this can be to a stage-struck kid?

There I was, all alone in the cold alley with the snow falling. I never ever saw the Yacknin girls again. But wherever they are I want them to know I forgive them.

And I wonder if Thelma Savada really got them to make that promise, or was it something she made up as a joke? Wherever you are, Thelma Savada, you can tell me the truth—*now!*

Another Merman incident, which took place on a New Year's Eve, comes back as an embarrassing memory every once in a while. I was older and in my senior year at high school. No longer did I stand in alleys waiting for Ethel Merman. But somehow I got my dates to take me to see current Merman shows.

On this particular New Year's Eve, my top-hatted, white-tied "smoothie" Harvard date, Norman Sond-heim, from Brookline, Massachusetts (all Harvard boys wore white ties and tails, then), got tickets to a Merman show.

As we sat there in our mezzanine seats a thought came to me. Since we were going to dance the New Year in at the Waldorf Astoria after the theatre, wouldn't it be a great idea to go backstage and in-vite Miss Merman and her date, whoever he might be, to join us? Since I was all dressed up and Norman was wearing tails and a top hat (and a cane!) I fig-ured the stage doorman would take us for part of the "right" crowd. And you know something? He did!

We got by him with ease. Fearless Harvard man Norman simply knocked on Miss Merman's dressing-room door. I stood off in a corner and watched as the door was opened by a gentleman in a dinner jacket. I recognized him from his pictures in the papers—he was the stockbroker.

I heard Norman inviting him and Miss Merman to join us at the Waldorf. The stockbroker, no doubt thinking this was a college-boy prank, was very polite and patient. He said that he and Miss Merman had other plans, but he appreciated the invitation. Then he gently closed the dressing-room door in my Har-vard boy's face. If my daughter went out with some-one who did what Norman did that New Year's Eve, I'd think he was a freak!

The years rolled by. I had my own radio show in New York and a couple of times, Ethel Merman would come on as a guest. We got to know each other professionally.

A friend of mine, the brilliant dancer and comedi-enne Betty Bruce had a part in Cole Porter's *Some-thing for the Boys* which starred Ethel Merman. It was through Betty that I became friendly with Ethel.

From time to time Betty would take me up for

visits to Ethel's apartment on Central Park West. And I would see Ethel at Sardi's or at a party.

When I knew Ethel Merman was coming to Detroit to star in *Gypsy*, I thought it would be fun to have a party for her. Naturally, I called her to ask if she'd like one and the idea delighted her. Betty Bruce was also in the cast of the touring *Gypsy*.

And now, here I was in Detroit sitting in a room filled with our friends at a party my husband and I were giving for Ethel Merman. And out there on the dance floor, Ethel Merman had sung and was now saying, "thank you" to her friends Shirley and Edward.

Until she reads this book—and I hope she does—Ethel Merman, I'm sure, doesn't have an inkling about those Saturday afternoons I stood in the cold alleys to see her. Or that my infatuation for show business was all started by that letter of introduction given me by Louis Sobol.

It's strange that I should have become a columnist—it wasn't what I started out to be. I wanted to be in the theatre. Well, maybe it isn't so strange at that, because it certainly has been my passport into show business.

If someone asks me what I majored in at Friends Seminary, I think my answer would have to be: "I majored in ETHEL MERMAN!"

# Embarrassing Moments

That big party we gave for Ethel Merman stands out as one of the great times in my life and also one of the most embarrassing ones.

First of all, because Ethel's big number in the show written by Jule Styne and Stephen Sondheim was "Rose's Turn," or as most people called it, "Everything's Coming Up Roses," we decided to cover the entire private Standard Club in the Sheraton Cadillac Hotel with real roses of every color and variety.

And I mean everywhere—they were to hang from the chandeliers, bandstand, on the buffet tables and in the centerpieces on all the individual tables.

The party was to take place on Saturday night because on Sunday Ethel could rest, with no performance to give that night.

All the flowers were to be delivered by Saturday morning. At some point on Friday, I talked to Benay Venuta, who is one of Ethel's closest friends and was also in the show. Fortunately, I mentioned that we had cornered the Detroit market on roses. "Oh, my God," exclaimed Benay. "You've got to get rid of all of them. Ethel is allergic to roses. Singing that song has been the scourge of her existence. Ever since

*Gypsy* opened on Broadway, she keeps getting tons of roses delivered to her dressing room which have to immediately be taken out. Ethel can't breathe or talk or sing if there are roses anywhere near her. They make her ill!"

This was Friday. The party was Saturday. What a hell of a predicament we were in! Sidney Shertzer, who does all the decorations for Detroit's Saks Fifth Avenue, was supervising the decorating as a special favor. Immediately I called to tell him of our plight. He sent out an SOS to scour all of Detroit for fake roses made of paper, silk, plastic and sugar. The florist canceled as many roses as possible with the green-houses. However, they couldn't unload all of them; the rest we had distributed in wards at a hospital.

Now let me tell you about a situation that could *not* be saved: our invitations called for guests to arrive from ten o'clock on. The buffet tables were laden down with gastronomic delights such as one whole section devoted to hot dogs, bologna, salami, pastrami and corned beef—all flown in from New York. Another section served beefsteak, curries and other hot foods, prepared by the excellent chef at the hotel. Still another part of the long table was devoted to all kinds of salads, from potato to Jell-o molds. And down at the end of the table were several dozen different kinds of gorgeous cakes and pastries, including cheese-cakes which were flown in from the famous Lindy's.

The chef at the Sheraton Cadillac, over a period of many years, had won first prize for his ice decorations. In the center of his table, molded in ice (thank God), was a huge bouquet of roses.

My husband had given strict orders to the maitre d' and the manager of the Standard Club to keep the food going the entire night, and the manager assured us that the waiters and chefs would be delighted with the overtime pay.

Most of the guests dined before the arrival of the

guest of honor and the other members of Ethel's *Gypsy* company. It wasn't possible for the cast to get there until close to midnight since the final curtain didn't ring down until 11:20.

Ethel arrived and seemed thrilled by the decorations, which included posters from every show in which she had ever starred—and hand-painted banners that read "Best Damn Actress—Ethel Merman in *Gypsy* (a direct quote from a New York critic) WELCOME TO DETROIT . . ." and was she ever relieved to discover that the thousands of roses all over the place were *fake*.

She was also very visibly moved by the standing ovation she received from the two hundred assembled guests.

Ethel sat at a table with Henry and Anne Ford. Because it was necessary to unwind after two shows that day, she drank some Dom Perignon before eating, and all the members of the cast also wanted a drink first.

Since it was midnight and many of the guests had been there from ten o'clock, Lyn Duddy, Joan Edwards and Jerry Bresler got up in the middle of the floor and began their specially prepared show with lyrics written to many of the tunes introduced and made famous by THE MERM. Some of them were hilarious—at her expense, of course. Others were sentimental and spoke of how adored and respected she was by both audiences and personal friends.

At the end of their tribute, in which they were aided and abetted by Carmel Quinn, Betty Bruce and Benay Venuta, the guests shouted for Ethel Merman to stand up and take a bow.

Ethel Merman did much more than that. She got up on the floor and sang. She was so great (when isn't she?) that people in Detroit are still talking about it a decade later.

Naturally everyone was turned toward the dance

floor where the show was taking place. The buffet table at this point was behind us at the other end of the room. When Ethel sat down after the show she said, "Now I'm hungry."

My husband took her by the arm to escort her to the food. He couldn't believe what he saw. Neither could I! The only thing left on the table was a seventy-five-foot, white tablecloth. It seems that the manager of the club had neglected to issue Edward's order to keep the food going the whole night long.

Apparently when the show started the waiters and captains, thinking everyone had already eaten, cleared off the table and had taken away every single bit of food.

Actors in shows seldom eat until after a performance, preferring not to work on full stomachs. So they were hungry. Do you see what I mean about one of my most embarrassing moments?

All that food plus the centerpieces of iced roses had disappeared into thin air. My husband, normally a quiet, gentle human being, blew his top!! He demanded that it all be brought back. There had been enough food for three parties.

Well, the manager assumed that everything had been put in the hotel's refrigerators. He ran down to the kitchen, only to come back to say that there was nothing there. Obviously, the waiters had already gone home and taken everything with them, maybe for parties of their own.

From New York we also had shipped by air, wheels of imported cheeses which had been on the dessert end of the table with the cakes. They too were gone. The only thing the manager could find to feed our hungry guest of honor was some American cheese, kept around, no doubt, to bait the hotel's mousetraps!

Someone went out to the nearest Coney Island and brought back some hot dogs and chili for Ethel and the *Gypsy* company to eat. The only thing I'm grateful for is that she did see the buffet table as she came into the room. At least she knew there had been food there.

I hope Ethel Merman by now has forgotten the stolen food caper. But even if she has—we never will!

# Where Scoops Come From

So often I am asked, "How do you, sitting in Detroit, get so many scoops?" For openers, I don't really stay in Detroit that much of the time.

Airline crews flying to New York, Los Angeles, London, Paris and Rome are beginning to consider me family; and lately, the airline "skyjack" friskers don't bother with me too much any more.

Even though I'm not away for more than six days at a time unless some part of my family is along, still, when I call home, my son says, "Mother who?"

Since it is the jet age, it's easier to go where the news is rather than wait for it to come to you. Maybe Elizabeth Taylor and Richard Burton won't let you in after you go all the way to Budapest to see them, but being kind to hotel floor maids can sometimes be just as gainful, newswise. Some of my best friends are hotel porters, maids and assistant chefs. The head chef never reveals anything about the tastes of his big famous and infamous tippers, but should they be less than generous he might squeal a little.

When I am at home in Detroit, a bulletin should be posted advising people of that fact, so they can then go out and buy large blocks of AT&T stock. I'm ashamed to tell anyone what our monthly phone bills come to, but when my husband speaks to his mother in New York for more than three minutes, I get mad. And *he* pays the bills! It's just that I might be missing a call from Danny Kaye's press agent, with something important and earth-shaking like "Danny had to go to the dentist today."

How do I get scoops? Well, here's an actual happening: A friend of mine, TV producer Michael Krauss, who was living in Chicago, called me in Detroit and said, "Have I got a scoop for you! Dustin Hoffman and his wife are expecting a baby."

Mrs. Hoffman already had a daughter from a former marriage. How did Mike in Chicago know what was going on with Dustin in New York? Well, Mike's mother, who lives in Detroit, has a friend named Millie Banowitz, who is a close friend of Mrs. Hoffman's (Dustin's mother), who lives in Los Angeles. Mrs. Hoffman, it seems, called Mrs. Banowitz long distance and said, "Millie, don't tell a soul, but my son's going to have a baby."

Mrs. Banowitz plays a card game called Pan with a group of "the girls" in Detroit. One of the girls in the game is Mrs. Krauss. During a schnecken and coffee break, Millie Banowitz told the girls (civilians all), never thinking it could possibly leak out to anyone in the communications field about the expected baby.

That night, Mrs. Krauss in Detroit called her son Michael in Chicago. Somewhere, in the course of conversation, she told him Millie Banowitz's news about the expectant Dustin Hoffmans.

Michael, being a good friend of columnist Shirley Eder in Detroit, called to tell her the news.

Twenty-four hours later, the headline in Shirley Eder's syndicated column shouted: "The Dustin Hoffmans Are Expecting." See how simple it is to get scoops? You just have to know relatives of the girls who play cards and coffee klatch at least once a week.

We'll never get news about Dusty that way again, because for some odd reason, Mrs. Hoffman doesn't confide in Millie Banowitz any more.

# Great Expectation

One of the biggest thrills of my life occurred while I was sitting in the Polo Lounge of the Beverly Hills Hotel with Academy Award nominee (*Midnight Cowboy*) Sylvia Miles, Earl Wilson and Houston columnist Maxine Mesinger. A call from publicist John Springer caught up with me at the table. He had arranged a date for me with his client Richard Burton at five-thirty that afternoon. "Okay," I said trying to be nonchalant, "I'll come over to bungalow 10," where the Burtons were in residence with their large retinue of secretaries and servants.

"No, don't do that," exclaimed Springer. "He's coming over to see you in your room." WOW!! Richard Burton coming to MY room!!

Immediately I called my husband at his Los Angeles office and told him not to dare to come home until after six, because Richard Burton would be with me.

Do you know what my husband said?

He said, "Thank goodness. Maybe now you'll throw out all those papers and clean up the place."

He sure was worried about Burton being in the bedroom alone with *me*, wasn't he?

It was only two o'clock, but I rushed back to clean up the room and change clothes two or three or four different times. What do you wear for Richard Burton? At three o'clock I called the Polo Lounge where Maxine Mesinger was still sitting with Earl Wilson and pleaded, "Please, Maxine, can you help me? I need help. I've been trying to get my false eyelashes on for thirty minutes, but it's no use, and now one is stuck way up on my right eyebrow."

In just minutes, my pal Maxine arrived with first aid in hand—a tube of Johnson's Eyelash Glue. She couldn't get over how neat the place looked. Even my typewriter had disappeared. She looked under the bed and, sure enough, it was there. I didn't think Richard and I would have to go *under* the bed for anything.

While Maxine was fiddling with my eyelashes, the phone rang. It was John Springer again, this time saying that Richard had thought it over and decided it might be advisable to meet in the Polo Lounge.

Was it possible Elizabeth was jealous of me? I'd like to think so.

Later, sitting with Richard Burton in the Polo Lounge watching him drink soda water and listening to his exquisitely modulated tones, I kept hoping that someone I knew from home would see us. No such luck. However, several of my fourth-estate pals sat smiling at me from a nearby table with pens and pencils in hand, pretending to copy everything they overheard. They were only kidding, but Richard has the kind of voice that booms out. He's used to projecting. If my buddies actually listened, this is what they heard:

SHIRLEY: It's strange seeing you drink soda water. What about these stories one reads about the amount of booze you consume?

RICHARD: Ah yes, the legend persists and it's not without some warrant. But for Henry VIII in *Anne of the Thousand Days* I deliberately put on twenty-five pounds which took me up to over 190. That's pretty bulky for five foot eleven, and I didn't like it very much.

SHIRLEY: How do you lose weight?

RICHARD: Primarily by not drinking. I eat well, steaks and eggs.

SHIRLEY: I must say you are much handsomer slim, the way you are now.

RICHARD: That's what Elizabeth says.

SHIRLEY: Elizabeth seems to be getting thinner too. (*Getting pretty chummy now calling her Elizabeth*). What's it like living in a glass house?

RICHARD: It's very difficult to say what it's like because I can no longer remember when it wasn't like this. It's been going on for so long. For Elizabeth, virtually, since she was a child. And for me, about fifteen years.

SHIRLEY: You seem to have so much, both of you. You certainly have been able to afford the world's most expensive jewels. Yet, is there possibly anything you don't have, that you really do want?

RICHARD: So many things that I really want have nothing to do with money. I'm writing a book at the moment—I'd like it to be successful. It's a kind of novel based on truth. Everything else goes fine with us. The children are all healthy and intelligent. Elizabeth's healthy and intelligent and quite good-looking (*the understatement of all time*).

SHIRLEY: Would you believe I worry about you? Have you put money away for that inevitable rainy "no work" day that comes to almost every actor?

RICHARD: Yes, it's already put away. We both could stop right now and would never have to work again. As a matter of fact, we did consider it for a time. But I don't think I could do it. The bug is too deeply in my blood and in Elizabeth's. I think we might semi-retire. That is to say, instead of doing film after film after film—as we have been doing—we'd make two films every three years. You know, we did take one year off. I didn't think I could last out, but we did.

SHIRLEY: Where do you make your home? Where do you vote?

RICHARD: I don't vote. I don't think there's anybody worth voting for. We have two houses I suppose we call home. One is in Switzerland high up in the Alps and the other is in Mexico. We have been thinking of one day perhaps living in Palm Springs. We went out to stay with Frank Sinatra. It's very attractive around there. So we're thinking about it. But there are so many tax questions and things like that which have to be resolved first.

SHIRLEY: You and Elizabeth, like Sinatra, seem to travel with an entourage of people. Do you ever just go someplace alone with Elizabeth?

RICHARD: You cannot go on a long journey alone. You simply can't. You have to have people with you to handle things. And when we work, we really need a staff. As a matter of fact, a lawyer in New York, who is also a very old friend of mine, has handled some of the biggest estates in the world, and he says that our various activities have a slightly bigger turnover than one of the newest African states.

SHIRLEY: Is it possible for the Burtons to have close friends?

RICHARD: We have several very close friends, which is rare in our profession. These people are loyal and close to us. They stuck by us during the great crisis. The era of *le scandale*, as I call it, which were the early days of Elizabeth and myself. Then you separated the men from the boys and found out who was your friend and who wasn't. We had the most extraordinary surprises! A girl friend of Elizabeth's, also a well-known film star, completely ignored us for six years. On the other hand, we had another friend, Mike Nichols, who was not as famous as he is now, but he was already well known as a theatre director. Mike just caught the next plane to Rome and came to hold our hands. Now, that is a friend! You'd be surprised how many people we knew would cut us in a restaurant. Of course, they're all back now, smiling like mad.

SHIRLEY: I hope you are cutting them!

RICHARD: No, I don't bother. I don't turn the other cheek, but I'm not as amiable and as affable towards them as I was before.

SHIRLEY: Are you very proud of your wife?

RICHARD: Yes, I am indeed!

SHIRLEY: What do you think it is that makes you both so exciting to other people?

RICHARD: I can't understand it because I'm a middle-aged man and Elizabeth is getting on to forty (*then*).

SHIRLEY: I don't think it's nice to tell a woman's age.

RICHARD: She doesn't mind. She's looking forward to middle age because she wants to play character parts. Her hair is going slightly gray and she won't even dye it.

SHIRLEY: Would you like her to?

RICHARD: No, I like her the way she is.

From here on in Mr. Burton's conversation was all about Mrs. Burton, which was a far cry from our original date—the assignation in this reporter's bedroom. Therefore, I refuse to waste any more space on this particular story!

# Katharine Hepburn
## and a Mother's Sacrifice

From the time our two children, Toni, now in her twenties, and John, eighteen, were tots, we always took them with us to the Beverly Hills Hotel for their Easter vacations. Their time off from school seemed always to mesh with the date of the Academy Awards, when I had to be there.

Toni, a really fine tennis player, has been pretty good at tennis since she was twelve. So most of her Easter vacation was spent on the hotel's tennis courts. She took lessons over the years from championship player Alex Olmeda. She was out on the courts early every morning and got to know most of the other regulars who took lessons from Olmeda.

Alex's first appointment in the morning was with Katharine Hepburn whenever she was in town. Toni became friendly with the elusive Kate, friendly to the extent of chatting with her about tennis, schools and things that a young teen-ager and a grownup might discuss together.

For years I had been trying to interview Katharine Hepburn—to no avail. She hates talking to the press. Her private life is her own business. When my daughter told me about her friend "Miss Hepburn," I suggested that she pave the way for an interview. Toni was aghast at the suggestion. "Mother," she cried. "Promise me you'll never bother Miss Hepburn. Please, make me that promise."

She was so sincere I could do nothing except promise never to infringe on her tennis friendship with Miss Hepburn.

I didn't promise, however, not to show up early in the morning to watch my daughter take her lesson, hoping, of course, for a miracle that would get me some kind of interview with the star.

Down to the tennis courts I would go, bleary eyed, about 8:45 A.M., to watch Kate swat that ball. And I mean *swat* it. I never saw anyone tear into a ball as hard or as vigorously as that lady. During the entire half-hour lesson she would shout out loud with joy when she won a point from the pro. And, equally as loud, she would castigate herself when she missed his serve or his return. She'd say things like "Kate, you old fool. How could you miss that one!"

Although it was very warm, with Los Angeles temperatures in the seventies, eighties and nineties, Kate Hepburn always played in a long-sleeve sweat suit. Lord knows she didn't do it to lose weight since she didn't have a spare ounce to lose.

From my daughter, I learned that the star was allergic to the sun and had to cover up from neck to sneaker to avoid the sun's rays. And this was her primary reason for playing early in the morning before the sun became too hot.

For several years at Eastertime I would sit on the sidelines just watching Toni talk with Katharine, without so much as a nod of recognition from my own daughter. A little offended by her attitude, I spoke to her about it. She said, "Mother, I don't want her to know you work for a newspaper." Honestly, I understood.

When Toni was a junior in high school, she and Miss Hepburn talked about Toni's choice of colleges.

The star filled my daughter in on her alma mater, Bryn Mawr. At the time, she obviously thought enough of Toni to tell her, "If you apply to Bryn Mawr and you need a letter of recommendation, I would be happy to write one for you." She even gave Toni her New York address.

It took a couple of years for Toni to have faith in her mother's integrity. But then one morning she actually introduced me to her "friend." Not by my maiden and pen name, "Shirley Eder," but quite properly by my married name.

After having graduated from Grosse Pointe University School, Toni chose to go to the University of Michigan. Once in college, she no longer vacationed with us in California. College girls, we learned, like to go off on their own.

Even though Toni wasn't with us, every once in a while I would go down to the tennis courts early enough to watch Kate Hepburn taking her lesson. One time she asked me how Toni was, and what school she had chosen and how she was doing. That was the extent of our conversation.

My daughter's brainwashing in the case of Miss Hepburn lingered on. I still felt duty bound to keep that promise I made to Toni about never approaching her friend for an interview.

The years went by and only after Toni had graduated from college did I write a column telling about the "promise" and how, because of it, I had never ever approached Katharine Hepburn for an interview. I sent a copy of the column to Alex Olmeda, who showed it to Miss Hepburn. Alex told me she smiled when she read it, but said nothing.

Miss Hepburn was always accompanied by a miniature German Shepherd or a dog that looked like a shepherd, who sat quietly on the sidelines, properly trained not to chase the balls. From my daughter I learned that the dog was given to Kate by "Spenc-ah," as the actress in her special New England accent called Spencer Tracy.

Toni didn't know, but I did, that some mornings at eight-thirty, Katharine Hepburn took diving lessons from the hotel's swimming instructor Sven Peterson. She chose that hour because the pool never officially opened before nine-thirty so at eight-thirty there were no other people there.

Somehow I learned about these lessons, and one time peeked through the slats of the closed gate and saw Miss Hepburn taking her diving lesson in the same sweat suit in which (after it dried out) she played tennis. If her dive wasn't particularly good, I heard her berate herself in the same manner as she did when she missed the ball in tennis.

Some two years ago when Katherine Hepburn was the toast of Broadway in *Coco,* Toni, now working in New York for the advertising company Ogilvy & Mather, made plans to see the show with a date.

She had kept the New York address which Miss Hepburn had given her years before, when she thought Toni might need a letter of recommendation. Toni wrote her a note. Forty-eight hours later she received an answer from Hepburn's long-time secretary, saying that Miss Hepburn was looking forward to seeing Toni again and would she come backstage after the performance, but please not to make it on a matinee day, when Miss Hepburn had two performances. Also in the letter were instructions as to how to find the stage door and the dressing room.

I think that's pretty neat! I mean for Hepburn to have remembered a young girl after so many years.

While Katharine Hepburn was making her last film with Spencer Tracy, *Guess Who's Coming to Dinner,* a top Columbia Pictures executive arranged for me to get on the set in spite of the sign which read "This Is an Absolutely Closed Set."

What a marvelous experience it was watching Tracy and Hepburn working together. It was tantamount to watching the greatest ballet or listening to the finest symphony music or watching the first take-off into space. Yes it was that thrilling. I was privileged, if only for a short while, to look in on perfection. Their teamwork was stunning.

I was told to stand out of camera range of the actors, which I did. Yet somehow, during a break, Miss Hepburn saw me out of the corner of her eye and instead of having me evicted, she smiled and waved. She probably thought I looked familiar. Or perhaps she did remember me as Toni's mother. It doesn't matter. It does matter that she was gracious.

P.S. Miss Hepburn, I still would like that interview!

# Barbara Stanwyck

Barbara Stanwyck was one of the few Hollywood superstars I had always wanted to interview, but until some twelve years ago, never could.

Finally, I managed to obtain an interview with her for NBC "Monitor." The meeting took place in the Hollywood office of her public relations woman and friend, Helen Ferguson. Helen was the rare press agent whose clients stayed with her for most of their working lives. She guarded their public and private lives with FBI-like secrecy; no one could pry from her anything she didn't want them to know. Over a period of years her list of clients included Clark Gable, Jeanette MacDonald, Gene Raymond, Loretta Young, Robert Taylor and Barbara Stanwyck.

Barbara is the rare star who doesn't want publicity. Unless she has something to say about her professional life, she refuses to be interviewed. She meets the press only to discuss the movie or the TV project on which she is currently working. She wants no personal publicity. When you know her well, you realize that she is a very private person. The reason Barbara okayed the interview with me at Helen's office was because at the time she was doing a weekly television show.

All of her meetings with the press take place somewhere outside her home. Helen Ferguson made it a point never to leave the room while one of her stars was being interviewed. She wanted to be sure she heard everything that went on the record.

It was lucky for me that, as I began to talk to Miss Stanwyck, Helen was called to her inner office for a long-distance call. It must have been important—she left me alone with Miss Stanwyck for forty-five minutes.

"Are you afraid," I asked, "of being interviewed alone?"

"Hell, no," replied the star. "If I find I don't like your tactics I'll use so many four-letter words your entire interview will be bleeped." And I knew she meant it. She very honestly went on to talk about the fact that motion-picture acting was becoming a man's profession: the majority of movie scripts were being written for male stars.

She was also very honest about saying that she was no longer being offered plum movie roles. Barbara's hair had turned gray at a young age, and she refused then—and still refuses today—to bleach or tint it any other color. I suggested that perhaps this was a deterrent to movie roles. She disagreed, saying the producers knew she would wear a blond wig as she had in *Double Idemnity*, the movie which earned her one of her four Academy Award nominations. "If they can't see it that way," she said, "the hell with them!" She was the most direct and honest actress I had ever met. I admired her instantly, as do most people who get the chance to meet her. "You know," she continued, "there was a time I thought of retiring from the whole acting business. I even went so far as to buy some paints and blank canvases. You know, you keep hearing people say that 'anyone can paint.' I tell you from experience that's a damn lie. When I found I couldn't work on canvas, I bought a very expensive 'paint by number' set. I could read the numbers, but

I swear I couldn't fill in the right places. Every kid can do it, but I can't!

"I'm not a very social person. I don't like to go to parties or entertain, except a few close friends. I do love to read. I read everything I can get my hands on and that's pretty good, considering I never got past the sixth grade. But you can't read twenty-four hours a day. You have to do something—so I continue to act."

Forty-five minutes later Helen burst back into the room saying, "I'm sorry I was away so long. Now we can start the interview." "Helen," laughed Barbara, "the interview is over and is already on tape." She sounded like a little girl saying: "Ha, this time I got away with it!"

"Well!" said Miss Ferguson. "Shirley, you'll stay and play the tape for me, won't you?" There was nothing on the tape that would hurt Barbara in any way, but I really didn't want to play it back. It was a good honest interview, and I didn't want anything changed.

"No, Helen," vehemently declared the star. "Shirley does not have to play the tape back for you. What's more, she has to leave now and so do I." Barbara winked at me victoriously, and we left the office at the same time.

You can bet Helen Ferguson called me at the hotel later to ask for a copy of that tape. I half promised to send her one, but somehow still have never gotten around to it.

Barbara Stanwyck, that day, endeared herself to me forever. She was so much "for real." I had never before come across an interviewee quite like her.

A year went by before our next meeting, which took place at a charity fashion show. Attending such an event was rare for her. But the clothes being shown were by Werle, who was her friend and also was the designer of all the clothes she wore on her anthology TV series. Barbara was there with Nancy Sinatra. I persuaded a mutual friend, Renee Godfrey to take me over to the Stanwyck-Sinatra table, although I was sure she wouldn't remember me. Renee started to say, "This is . . . ," but she didn't have to continue because Barbara immediately said: "Shirley Eder. I remember you and I hope you never did send Helen Ferguson that tape."

When Barbara Stanwyck works, she absolutely never socializes. Possibly at the end of a work week she might ask a friend in to dinner or perhaps go out to Chasen's. Renee Godfrey, the wife of one of Barbara's favorite directors, Peter Godfrey, often had dinner on Friday nights with Barbara. Her husband had been ill for years with Parkinson's disease.

I don't know how Renee worked it, but I shall be forever grateful to her and to her memory (she died several years ago from cancer) because she managed to get me invited to Barbara's house *After* dinner one Friday evening. And that was the start of what I hope will be a lifetime friendship.

I can hear Barbara saying now, as I came through the front door that night, "I don't know what you're doing here. I never let press come into my house!" Apparently some sixth sense told her that once I came through her front door, nothing that I ever heard in her house would reach print without her express permission. For some reason she trusted me. That's the kind of trust one hopes never to betray.

Those closest to Barbara Stanwyck call her "Missy." Sometime during the evening of that first visit she asked me to call her Missy.

Remembering that during our interview she mentioned that she had worn for many years only one perfume, Tuvache's Jungle Gardenia, I bought a small bottle of it to give to her.

I have since learned that you can never give Barbara a gift without immediately receiving one in return. That first night she disappeared from the room for about ten minutes, coming back carrying a cream-colored short evening dress on a monogrammed hanger. "Here," she said, handing me the dress, "I'd like you to have this." I was embarrassed and said I couldn't accept such an expensive present. "It isn't second-hand," she protested. "I had it made for myself and haven't worn it yet. Please take it. I want you to have it."

It was given so much from the heart I couldn't refuse. As she took us to the door when it was time to leave, she laughed and said, "Please send the hanger back. I can't afford to have new monogrammed hangers made!"

I never wore that beautiful dress for a very sad reason. You see, Barbara Stanwyck weighed a hundred and two pounds and I weighed—well, a hell of a lot more! I do, however, still have the dress. It's been put away in tissue paper and moth balls and packed in a special box. Perhaps one day I'll give it to Debbie Reynolds for her Motion Picture Museum.

# She Didn't Think
# the Young People Cared

There are only a handful of superstars who can
cause a real commotion walking down a street in New
York. Barbara Stanwyck is one of those. Barbara, who
hadn't been in New York in some twelve years, in
1965 went with my husband and me for some ten
days of shopping, theatregoing and just walking
through the Central Park Zoo (one of her favorite
places in the world).

On Fifth Avenue, heads turned as we walked. Small
armies of people gathered, following us from store to
store. I say "us," but you know they were following
Barbara. They waited in large groups outside the
Plaza Hotel, where we were staying, just to get a
glimpse of her.

There was always excitement when we went to the
theatre. The first show we saw was *Golden Boy* starring Sammy Davis, Jr. As we walked down the theatre
aisle to our seats fifteen minutes before the curtain
was to go up (Barbara never comes late to the theatre), you could hear the hum of voices growing louder and louder. The three of us looked around to see
what was happening. The voices came from the balcony, the orchestra, from all over the theatre. Pretty

soon we heard the hum turn into the name "Barbara Stanwyck."

Barbara sat rigidly in her seat, not knowing what to do. For some reason she seemed shocked by so much attention. When the curtain went up the calling of her name stopped, and the audience became involved in the show.

Then at intermission, people stood up, but we seemed to be the only ones walking up the aisle. From the balcony came the call "Barbara Stanwyck, look up here. Please look up here." She looked up and waved. Then, one by one, and group by group, everyone in the theatre stood up together. Suddenly the entire theatre began to applaud her. Barbara was visibly moved by this demonstration.

It was raining that night, so during the intermission she stood in the inside lobby signing autographs and shaking hands. Just as we were to return to our seats, a group of rain-bedraggled young fans pushed their way into the lobby handing her a bouquet of roses, which they had obviously run out to buy somewhere on Broadway. These young people were not ticketed members of the audience. I watched Barbara when they handed her the wet flowers. Tears rolled down her cheeks. As we walked back to our seats she whispered, "You know, I didn't think the young people really cared." Then she laughed and said, "Maybe it pays to stay away for such a long time. I better not show up in New York City for another twelve years."

When the curtain came down, an emissary, sent by Sammy Davis, Jr., asked if Miss Stanwyck would come backstage. When we walked through the stage door, from the inside of the theatre, the entire cast of *Golden Boy* stood in a line on the stage and applauded. I've been backstage with many stars, but never before heard this kind of applause from an assembled cast.

Several nights later, walking out of the Winter Garden Theatre after *Mame*, hundreds of people gath-

ered around Barbara Stanwyck in the outside lobby
wanting her to sign autographs. She might be there
still if it hadn't been for the fact that the show's company manager came over and said, "Miss Stanwyck,
if you don't let us close the theatre, we have to pay
overtime to the ushers, porters, etc."

"I'm in television," she replied. "I know what overtime can cost."

So out to the street she went, continuing the auto-
graphing session for another forty minutes. Snow had
begun to fall on her uncovered white hair. The crowds
waiting for her signature never noticed.

Much later, back in our suite at the Plaza, we spent
most of what was left of that night talking. Sitting with
her feet up on the window ledge over the radiator,
looking out over the deserted Wollman skating rink,
watching the snow turn Central Park into the kind of a
scene you'd like to own on canvas, Barbara said wist-
fully, "You know, Shirley, I can remember when I was
poor—oh, so poor and so cold because my coat was too
thin to give warmth. But as cold as I was, I loved being outside when the first winter snow fell on New
York City. It was magic time for me then, and it's still
magic, except now, with my feet on this radiator, I'm
so nice and warm."

That night Barbara told me how, at the height of
her movie fame, when her hair was a reddish brown,
she could walk all over New York City and go to the
theatre and seldom be recognized. I couldn't believe
this. "It's true," she said. "Believe it or not, it's the
white hair that has made me so easily recognizable."
Perhaps that was partially true. But can you imagine
Barbara Stanwyck walking down a New York street
totally unnoticed? I can't.

And can you imagine the kind of excitement created
when she went walking down Fifth Avenue on the
arm of her husband, Robert Taylor? Oh, I can!

# A Visit from a Star Chez Moi

Just in case "a Barbara Stanwyck" comes to stay at your house, here are a few hints on what to expect.

For openers, you look around the house you have lived in and loved and ignored for so many years, and you realize the carpet in your son's room is worn out, the tile floor in your kitchen needs repairs, your husband's chair is sagging and all your curtains need cleaning.

It's amazing how, in less than a week, just by dropping the name of your famous guest, you manage to get the upholsterer, the laundress, the carpeting laid and the tile repaired—as a matter of fact, almost the whole house redone.

Then, while she is in residence, the phone never stops ringing with invitations to lunch at city clubs, country clubs, expensive restaurants, dinner parties small and large and drives into the country to see the changing colors of the leaves (if it should be in the fall).

Then come the calls from the local radio and TV broadcasters saying, "I'd like you to drop in just to say hello on my show and, by the way, feel free to bring your house guest. We can always clear time for her."

Then comes a shopping and browsing tour through your favorite stores. You have dark glasses. Your guest not only doesn't wear dark glasses, but neither does she wear makeup, except for a little lipstick. She is stopped every few feet for a handshake or an autograph.

Your husband puts on his best suit early in the morning and in the evening dons the smoking jacket you gave him fifteen years ago, but has never worn because at the time he said he's not "that" kind of guy! Your children are so polite you think there has been a mix-up and you got the neighbors' kids instead of your own.

Your faithful poodle, whom you have seen through illness and carpet wetting and vet bills since she was a pup, jumps up on the sofa into the arms of your celebrated guest sneering at you, knowing she is on "off limits" territory and daring you to do something about it in front of "you know who."

The doorbell rings constantly with harbingers bearing flowers and candy and someone's homemade chicken soup and someone else's special lobster goo. All these things naturally are delivered in person by the people who have prepared them. Then, just as naturally, you invite them in for a visit. Your guest smiles and is always charming, while you keep making fresh pots of coffee and defrosting Sara Lee's best.

"A Barbara Stanwyck" has probably come to your town for a United Foundation or community drive where she is a guest speaker. For the very first time in all the years you have worked so faithfully for the same organization, you are asked to sit at the speakers' table too.

This might sound like a disgruntled hostess, but let me tell you something. I don't know about "a" Barbara Stanwyck, but when it's the Barbara Stanwyck,

# SHIRLEY IN WONDERLAND
## A PHOTOHISTORY

"Not this time, Cary Grant..."

"Yes, this time, Edward Slotkin..." Our wedding
with the two matrons of honor, Nancy Kelly and Mitzi Green.
(Photo by Eve Harrison)

With Van Johnson—in a Sally Victor hat (**sans** hatbox, this time).

Our **Camelot** party for Kathryn Grayson, who is flanked by
Edward and our daughter, Toni.

I told you Elizabeth Taylor didn't care whom
she talked to the night she won the Oscar for **Butterfield 8**
in 1960. By then she was Mrs. Eddie Fisher.

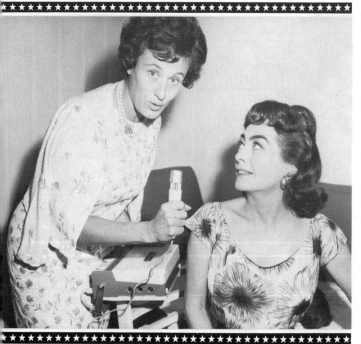
On the set of **Straightjacket** with Joan Crawford in 1963.
(Photo by Christie, Columbia Pictures Corp.)

Ginger Rogers and this reporter on the golf course in Detroit. (I promptly gave up tennis forever and took up golf after the fiasco on Ginger's tennis court.)

BEST
DAMN
ACTRESS
ETHEL MERMAN
in GYPSY

WELCOME
TO
DETROIT

At our party for Ethel Merman when she came
to Detroit in **Gypsy** in 1960. Who would dream she was
allergic to roses! (Photo by Rod Reiser)

With the Dustin Hoffmans—before Millie Banowitz
spilled the beans!

Interviewing gorgeous and young Richard Burton
during the filming of **The Bramble Bush** at Warner Brothers in
1959. (And to think he hadn't even met Liz Taylor yet!)

With Elvis Presley and Barbara Stanwyck on the set of
**Roustabout** in 1963. (Colonel Parker, his erstwhile manager, was
in the picture too, but insisted upon being airbrushed out.)

With Carol Channing and Jule Styne, composer of **Lorelei**, around the piano when **Lorelei** came to Detroit in March 1973.

A publicity still with "costar" Troy Donahue in the movie
**Palm Springs Weekend** in 1962.

FUN ON THE RUN!

# PALM SPRINGS WEEK·END

*in Technicolor!*

*Starring*

TROY DONAHUE ⋆ CONNIE STEVENS
TY HARDIN ⋆ STEPHANIE POWERS
and JERRY VAN DYKE *with*
Detroit's Own SHIRLEY EDER

STARTS WEDNESDAY

The way my motion picture debut was promoted in the
big downtown Detroit theatre. Pretty good billing for just
three lines! (Photo by R. K. Arnold, newspictures)

Lana Turner and this reporter on the set of **The Survivors**—
which didn't (but Lana did).

The eternally young Mae West on the set of **Myra Breckinridge.**
So how come they forgot to touch up my face too?

With Baroness Nina Van Pallandt and her manager at **The Godfather** première party at the St. Regis Hotel in New York in 1972, soon after she ''sang'' (about Clifford Irving).

With Barbra Streisand—and to think "hot dogs"
were the key to success in getting that first interview with her.
(Photo by Columbia Pictures)

Here's a switch: Eder interviewing the great Walter Winchell.

Talking to La Dietrich (at least we **looked** like we were talking).
(Photo by Allen Malschick)

On the set of **The Love Machine** with Jacqueline Susann,
author of the novel from which the movie was made. (Photo by
Columbia Pictures Industries, Inc.)

My first guest shot on the "Mike Douglas Show,"
with comedienne Joan Rivers, actor Richard Deacon, the
fabulous Gloria Swanson and Mike himself.

A truly historic occasion—Fred Astaire and
Ginger Rogers' first public appearance together in years at the
Academy Awards. I was delighted to be on that scene.

With sexy "Haps" (that's what his parents call their son Burt) Bachrach. (Photo by the Westbury Studio)

At the Plaza Hotel in 1971 with handsome John Lindsay, Mayor of New York City, and I. Robert Kriendler, president of the famed "21" Club. (Photo by Sam Siegel, Metropolitan Photo Service, Inc.)

No one could tell that supertalented Diana Ross was pregnant at the time but I knew. Here we are with Tom Jones at Tom's Caesars Palace opening in 1971. (Photo by Las Vegas News Bureau)

"And that's my daughter, Toni…" who for years stood between me and Katharine Hepburn.

Sharing the spotlight with Tricia Nixon Cox at the
Dinah Shore show in 1972.

On the set of MGM's **Soylent Green** with Edward G.
Robinson, a special and good friend, shortly before his death
in 1973. This, his 101st movie, was to be his last.

you don't mind anything because she's the kind of friend they just don't make any more. And even more than that, she has definitely become a part of your family. Who says you can't choose your relatives!

# The Robert Taylor Funeral

For the twelve years Robert Taylor and Barbara Stanwyck were married, they were idolized as a couple by the moviegoing public. The fan magazines continually wrote about their idyllic marriage. You can imagine how shook up those millions of fans were by the Stanwyck-Taylor separation and subsequent divorce.

Several years after the divorce, Bob Taylor married a lovely looking German actress named Ursula Thiess. Barbara has never married again.

When Robert Taylor died from lung cancer, Barbara was devastated, as were legions of people who either knew him personally or from his many years as a star in motion pictures and television.

Barbara found it difficult to make the decision to attend his funeral. She definitely did not want a three-ring circus made of the fact that she, his former wife, was there. She felt that, after all, she had not been Mrs. Robert Taylor for many years, and yet she wanted very much to go.

When the funeral plans had been made by his family, Barbara received a phone call from their mu-

tual long-time business manager Morgan Maree, saying Ursula wanted her to be there.

Not until the morning of the funeral could Barbara
make up her mind to go. When she did, she deliberately wore a yellow suit, feeling that the privilege
of wearing black belonged not to her but to the present Mrs. Robert Taylor.

Barbara was escorted to the funeral service at For-
est Lawn by Andy Maree, Morgan's son. Ursula Taylor,
with her two children, came with Morgan and Bob's
closest friend, from the time they started as actors
together, California's Governor Ronald Reagan.

Barbara declined Ursula's invitation to join them in
the "family room," feeling it might be difficult for Ursula to explain to her two children just who Barbara
was and why she was sitting with them. So she sat out
in the chapel with the other mourners.

She tried so hard to keep from crying. As disci-
plined as she normally is, this was something she could
not help. Too many memories flashed through her
mind as Ronald Reagan, from the pulpit, spoke about
his friend.

At the end of the service, dozens of world-wide
television newsreel photographers waited outside to
grab pictures of the long parade of celebrities. Barbara
left the chapel on the arm of Andy Maree. In spite of
the dark glasses, you could see the tears still running
down her cheeks as they went to their car. I saw this
as I watched the news that night on television, back
in Detroit.

As she was getting into the car, Morgan Maree came
over to her, she told me, saying, "Ursula insists you
come back to the house."

Barbara protested, arguing that she didn't think it
was right for her to go home with Bob's family. She
was then told that if she didn't come back to the
house, Ursula said she would come herself to get her.
She did not want Barbara to go home to cry alone.

There was nothing for Barbara to do but to accept Ursula's touching invitation.

When she walked into Robert Taylor's Manderville Canyon home, Ursula held her arms out to her and hugged her close, saying, "Bob's two wives."

The two Mrs. Taylors went off together to the garden where they talked and cried on each other's shoulder.

Before she left to go home, Barbara said to Ursula, "God love you and your children."

Many months after the funeral, their mutual business office delivered to Barbara a package of things that had belonged to Bob, who apparently had requested that they be sent to Barbara upon his death; he knew at the time that he had cancer.

In that package were several pieces of gold jewelry, including two money clips, a platinum and gold cigarette case that Barbara had given to Bob before they were married, a gold cigarette lighter with an inscription that read "To Lt. Robert Taylor with my admiration and my love from Mrs. Robert Taylor," and a photograph album filled with pictures of the two of them taken on their first trip together to Europe.

When Barbara received these familiar objects, she once again broke down and cried. They brought back memories. Obviously, although they had been divorced for so many years, he did love her enough to save these sentimental remembrances.

Barbara had one of the money clips put on a chain for me to wear around my neck. Seldom do I go without it.

She gave the other money clip to my daughter, Toni, because Bob was born on August 5, and Toni on August 3, and this clip bears the emblem of their astrological birth sign Leo the Lion.

She gave my son, John, Robert Taylor's lighter, which now has the additional inscription: "To John with love from Barbara Stanwyck."

My children love and adore Barbara. While they

were growing up, she never spoke down to them. She always treated them with respect, and in return is respected by them.

I know for a fact that Toni and John will cherish these keepsakes all of their lives, as did Robert Taylor, whether or not he ever carried them after the divorce.

There were several magazine stories here and abroad written about the Robert Taylor funeral, in which Barbara Stanwyck was chastised for wearing bright yellow. Little did the writers or readers of these stories realize that she wore a bright color deliberately out of the deepest respect for the widow, whose right it was to be dressed in black. Nor do people know that when Barbara Stanwyck returned to her own home after the funeral, she threw that yellow suit (which was brand new) down the incinerator, never wanting to see it again.

What a fortunate man Robert Taylor was, to have had in his lifetime two great ladies as wives. And, you know something? I believe he knew this. I also think he loved them both—always.

# Lunch with Not One,
# But Two Superstars

Although Barbara Stanwyck and Joan Crawford have been good friends ever since their reign as two of the most important stars in motion pictures, they seldom see each other. Joan moved to New York when she married Alfred Steele (then head of Pepsi Cola), and Barbara still lives in Beverly Hills.

When Joan heard that Barbara was visiting in New York with us, she called and invited Barbara and me to "21" for lunch. Barbara Stanwyck, normally a strong-willed lady with a definite mind of her own, is a minor leaguer in "will" department compared to Joan.

When the captain at "21" came to take the lunch order, Joan did the ordering for the three of us. Saying, "You both like calves liver, don't you!" Not waiting for answers, she ordered calves liver for three. She also chose our vegetables and the salad, leaving only the choosing of the dessert to us. Naturally, the two movie stars didn't eat dessert, which shamed me into saying, "None for me either."

When Joan got up from the table to greet someone in another part of the room, Barbara said, "I hate calves liver."

"Why don't you tell her?" I asked.

"I wouldn't dare!" she said. I don't like calves liver either, but if Barbara Stanwyck didn't have the guts to speak up and say, "No thank you," I certainly didn't!

That day before going to "21," Joan asked us to meet her at her fantastic Fifth Avenue duplex apartment. She wanted Barbara to see it; I had been there before. While showing us around, she took us up the stairs to the master bedroom. Barbara was most surprised to see a tiny framed picture of herself nestled among other photographs of family and friends on the night table. Even though they hadn't seen each other for so many years, Joan thought enough of Barbara to have kept a photograph of her for all that time.

Since then, Joan has moved from the penthouse to another apartment in New York. I'm told by those who have been in the new apartment that Barbara's picture is still right there on Joan's night table.

The girls saying "good-by" that day after lunch at "21" vowed they would definitely never permit another umpteen years to pass again without seeing each other.

Several months later, Joan wrote Barbara a letter saying she would be in California to do a TV show and asked Barbara to have dinner with her, if possible, the night she arrived.

Barbara answered the letter at once saying she would certainly save the date and was looking forward to dinner.

On the morning of the arrival day, Barbara received a phone call from Joan's California secretary, Betty Barker. Ms. Barker said, "Miss Stanwyck, Miss Crawford is in flight from New York to Los Angeles. Before she left for the airport, she asked me to call you to ask you to meet her at Don the Beachcomber's for dinner at 5 P.M."

"Five P.M.!" exclaimed Barbara. "Who eats dinner

at that ungodly hour? Why do we have to meet so early?"

"Miss Stanwyck," continued the secretary, "Miss Crawford's stomach will be on Eastern Standard Time."

"Well," said Missy Stanwyck, "you tell Miss Crawford that Miss Stanwyck's stomach is on California time and has been on California time for the last thirty years."

Needless to say, these two superstars did not have dinner together that night—nor have they dined together since!

Yet, believe it or not, they do correspond from time to time. There is mutual admiration and respect between them. Perhaps if they lived in the same town, they would see more of each other, perhaps not. It's simply that in their world, unlike ours, there is often no time to see the people they love. But I do know this: One could call on the other for help if and when it was ever needed. It's a strange friendship, but nevertheless, it's real.

# An "I Told You So" Tale

*Hello, Dolly!*, starring Carol Channing, produced by David Merrick and directed by Gower Champion, opened its pre-Broadway trial period at the Fisher Theatre in Detroit on November 18, 1963.

I remember so well Charles Lowe, Carol's husband and manager, calling me the day of the preview performance.

He said, "Shirley, how many laughers do you know?"

I didn't know what he meant by "laughers." He explained that he wanted me to gather together some six or eight friends to come as his guests to the preview, providing I could guarantee they would laugh out loud.

Never having tested any of my friends for their laughability quotient, I told him I'd have to see what I could do.

Immediately I started a phone campaign. After some thirty or more "you must be kidding" answers re the "laughing" bit, I managed to gather together my teen-age daughter, my sister-in-law, her daughter-in-law and a couple of odd-ball friends. All women.

I could get no guaranty from a man that he would laugh.

Charlie sat in the seat on the aisle. I sat next to him with my laughers alongside in the same row. But it was difficult to laugh—the performance that night was a disaster. The scenery didn't work, the music drowned out the singers, lines were forgotten and the body mikes boomed out and zonked out as did the amplifying system. So help me, that preview audience turned into nineteen hundred mourners and six laughers. Although nothing came off really funny, when Charlie laughed, I nudged my daughter to nudge the others down the line, and we all laughed with him. I wonder how we sounded to the rest of the audience?

The next night *Hello, Dolly!* opened officially. At the time, I was doing sixty-second reviews of plays and movies on the 11 P.M. news on WJBK-TV, an affiliate of CBS. The opening-night performance was definitely less disastrous—at least the scenery worked and most other technical defects had been remedied. However, the show itself wasn't very much better.

But Carol Channing was brilliant! Despite a death-like response from the audience, I had a "gut" feeling that the show, with a whole lot of fixing, would be a smash hit. I based this premise on four things—Carol Channing, the "Waiter's Gallop," the "Hello, Dolly!" number and that master director-choreographer Gower Champion.

During opening night intermission I chatted with the newspaper critics from Detroit's two daily newspapers, the Detroit *Free Press* and the Detroit *News*. They didn't come out and say it, but by what they did *not* say I knew they hated the show. I also spoke with the Detroit stringer for the show-biz bible, *Variety*. His opinion of the show was more important than the local newspaper reviews. If *Variety* gave it a good out-of-town notice, theatre parties in New York would then book the show in advance. If he didn't like it, it would hurt the benefit sales and these parties have become the backbone of the Broadway theatre. The rising costs of theatre make the price of a ticket too expensive for the average Broadway playgoer and unless word of mouth up front about a show is great, or unless *The New York Times* gives it a positive review he is afraid to take a chance on a show.

*Variety*'s reviewer liked Carol Channing but wasn't too crazy about the show. We discussed the parts he did like and those he didn't like.

Just before the opening-night curtain came down, I had to rush off to do my sixty-second TV review. I gave the show a qualified rave, singing the praises of Gower Champion's brilliant direction, Carol Channing's never-to-be-forgotten performance, the "Hello, Dolly!" number and the "Waiter's Gallop." Also, in just that one minute, I said that there was much doctoring needed. Since *Dolly* was to stay out on the road for several more weeks before it opened in New York, I felt there was plenty of time to work the show into a hit.

By the time I arrived at the opening-night party, given across the street from the threatre at Topinka's (the Sardi's of Detroit), word had reached those concerned about my qualified "rave" review.

When I came through the door, there was a scattering of applause simply for what I said about the show. Naturally I was pleased and felt like a celebrity as everyone gathered around me including the New York press representatives (Solters and Sabinson) for *Dolly*. Oh yes, I felt pretty special, until David Merrick, whom I had never met, came up to me unsmiling and looking very much like a villain with his black mustache and said, "I suppose you think you did us a favor with your review of *Hello, Dolly!*. Now everyone in it will think they have a hit so they'll sit back and take it easy instead of working harder."

Smiling, but not with my eyes, I looked up at "Mr. Mustache" and replied, "Mr. Merrick, you don't have a thing to worry about. Just wait till you read tomorrow's papers." I knew the show would get clobbered.

Charles Lowe and the New York press agents heard me and immediately asked if I knew what the man from *Variety* thought of it? Did he like it?

I told them what he had said to me during intermission. How he felt about the second act, I didn't know. They asked if there was any way I could find out that night. Well, I remembered his saying that he had to run to the Western Union office as soon as the curtain came down to write and wire his review into weekly and daily *Variety*. (Daily *Variety* is important to the movie colony.)

The press agents and Charles Lowe emptied their pockets of nickels and dimes, which they handed to me, while pushing me into a pay phone booth.

Discovering that the office downtown was the only Western Union open at that hour, I called to ask if so-and-so was there. The operator said that there was a man sitting at a desk using one of their typewriters. I knew that man had to be our man.

He came to the phone thinking something terrible had happened at home. It was past midnight and only his family knew where he was. But he told me in substance what his review would say. I repeated it word for word, as he was telling it, to those crowded in and around the phone booth. Well, the word wasn't very good!

*Variety*'s man in Detroit was a man of integrity and honor, and I knew he couldn't be made to change his mind. So, for almost an hour, I stayed in that telephone booth with the others breathing down my neck (à la a Marx Brothers movie), telling him how I felt about *Hello, Dolly!* and why I thought it would be a smash hit in New York. He listened—we argued—I felt he should put the good things at the top of his review with the negative points later. And, if possible, I thought he should explain how he thought those things he didn't like could be fixed or even eliminated.

By now, he was beaten down by the long conversation, and he had a deadline to meet. He said he would think again about possibly rearranging his criticism, although he definitely would write what he didn't like about the show.

The next day, as I expected, the newspaper reviews crucified the show. The critics counted *Hello, Dolly! out!*

A day or so later the review in *Variety* said at the beginning of the story that Carol Channing was great and her *Hello, Dolly! could* be a smash hit. He then went on to tell what was good about the show, and concluded with his very constructive criticism.

And the *Variety* critic's review was at least in part responsible for the advance sale of one million dollars' worth of tickets in charity benefits to *Hello, Dolly!*. Charles Lowe, Carol Channing, Gower Champion, the rest of the cast and the press agents were overjoyed.

Before that review, Mr. Merrick had wanted to close the show in Detroit. Charlie Lowe and Gower Champion had a Canadian syndicate of money men who were willing to take over the production from Merrick. And when "Mr. Mustache's" bluff, if it was a bluff, about closing the show was called, he changed his mind.

Word of mouth about *Hello, Dolly!* in Detroit was bad. Business at the box office had been hurt by the local reviews. And then after a few weeks into its run, President Kennedy was assassinated. Certainly no one felt like going to the theatre at the time; the country went into mourning.

Gower, Carol and everyone else with the show continued to work all hours of the day and night. When *Hello, Dolly!* left Detroit, it had been improved. Still, most of the reviews were not what you would call raves. They were, however, much better than the Detroit notices.

I always had the feeling that the show eventually would open as a hit in New York. I couldn't go to the

Broadway opening since we were in California at the time. But how well I remember the morning after it opened. We were sitting by the pool at the Beverly Hills Hotel, and I received two calls—one from Carol Channing and Charles Lowe, and the other from Marge and Gower Champion. Both told us that the New York critics had flipped for *Hello, Dolly!* and the lines waiting to buy tickets at the St. James Theatre on West 44th Street were already formed halfway down the block.

*Variety*'s man in Detroit and Shirley Eder became "wunderkinds" to many of the people connected with the show; everyone else had guessed wrong.

Any time Charlie Lowe sees me at a party or in a restaurant he announces to everyone within earshot, "Shirley Eder is the one who practically singlehandedly saved *Hello, Dolly!* from disaster." That isn't exactly true! I may have helped the *Variety* critic to see the light about rearranging his paragraphs, but it was Gower Champion's ingenious direction and Carol Channing's fantastic insight into the role of Dolly Levi that made *Hello, Dolly!* the second longest running Broadway musical of all time. Only *Fiddler on the Roof* beat its record.

When *Hello, Dolly!* opened the first time in Detroit, there was never a line at the box office waiting for tickets, but several years later when Carol Channing returned to that city as a part of her national tour, it was an entirely different story!

I remember the Sunday ad, some two months ahead of its arrival, announcing that the box office was now open for *Dolly* tickets. It was a cold and snowy Sunday, but that did not deter thousands who came down to the Fisher Theatre to purchase tickets at a much higher price this time. Not only did an entire extra staff have to be put on at the box office, but security guards were hired inside and outside the building to keep order.

The first day the tickets went on sale, the box office

opened at 8 A.M. and stayed open until past midnight. The Fisher Theatre is in a high-rise office building. The restaurant in it, Al Green's, which is normally closed on Sundays, opened its kitchen just to make hot coffee to keep the crowds who stood in line from freezing.

And the Nederlander family who own the theatre saw to it that boxes upon boxes of doughnuts were brought in and distributed to the waiting ticket buyers. Maybe they didn't want their potential customers starving to death before they reached the box office with the loot in hand. The whole scene looked like a disaster area with the Red Cross feeding the starving people.

The second time around for Carol Channing and *Hello, Dolly!* was like the "second coming." All of Michigan was at her feet and on their feet, giving her a standing ovation at each performance. Needless to say, this time Charles Lowe did not call on me to bring in a group of laughers. The laughers came on their own.

One final note: David Merrick, I'm sure, has blocked from his memory the fact that he wanted to close *Hello, Dolly!* before it moved from Detroit. What's more, not only has he never acknowledged my small part in helping *Hello, Dolly!*, but no matter how many times we meet (and we meet often), he never remembers me. We keep getting reintroduced.

I don't care if he never gets to know me or my name; I just want him to continue producing plays. He's one of the few people left with the guts to take a chance. The theatre definitely needs "Mr. Mustache," David Merrick.

# The Star Who Came to Dinner

Inviting Carol Channing to your home for dinner is a fascinating experience. We asked Carol and her husband Charles Lowe to come to our home in Detroit for dinner on her Sunday night off. No big deal—just our family and the Lowes.

About a week before the dinner, I had several phone calls with Charlie Lowe which went something like this:

"Hello, darling, this is Charles. What kind of carpeting do you have in your house?"

"Expensive!" I quickly exclaimed.

"I didn't mean that," he continued. "Is it wool or nylon or is it made of some other synthetic fiber? You see, Shirley, Carol is allergic to certain kinds of materials."

I made a long-distance call to New York to the decorator who some twelve years earlier had ordered the carpet for us. When I reported to Charles that it was made of wool, he said it wasn't exactly right, but for one evening it might not be too harmful.

Another call—

"Shirley, what kind of water do you take in your house?"

I explained that it was just plain old tap water donated to us by the city. Well, it wasn't actually donated since we pay water bills every month.

Charles then explained that Carol was permitted to drink only bottled water, and only a brand called Mountain Valley. I was relieved to find that I didn't have to climb a mountain with a bucket in hand to catch rain water on the top. Charlie said, "You can buy it by the bottle in a grocery store." I agreed to run out and buy a gallon jug as soon as we hung up.

"Darling," said Charles, "Carol drinks two gallons of water in between dinner and bedtime." (And *she did*.)

When Hildegarde became the spokesman for Mountain Valley Water I couldn't understand how the Lowes let her get away with this lucrative coup. But I'm glad they did, because Hilde does a great job for Mountain Valley Water.

The day before the Sunday Carol and Charlie were expected chez nous, the phone rang. It was Charles. This time he asked, "What kind of stove do you have?"

When I ashamedly told him it was over ten years old, he said, "I don't care if it's fifty years old. I just want to know if it is electric or gas."

Thank God, it was electric because he told me she wasn't permitted to eat anything cooked by gas (my apologies to Michigan Gas Co.). Perhaps after reading this the Detroit Edison will put in gratis just two much-needed burners on top of our old stove.

On Sunday morning another call came from Charles. "Shirley, do you ever drink cranberry juice? If not, we can bring you some. You see, Carol and I drink that instead of cocktails."

For some strange reason we had a large bottle of cranberry juice in the fridge. Maybe it was left over from a past Thanksgiving.

I figured I should tell Charles exactly what the menu was going to be in case Carol was allergic to

135

anything on it. We were having a thick soup, steak, stuffed baked potatoes, spinach ring, tossed endive salad and chocolate soufflé for dessert.

"That sounds great," said the exuberant Charles.

"You mean," I asked, stunned, "Carol isn't allergic to anything on that menu?"

"Oh," he replied, "she's allergic to every single thing you're having. But don't be concerned because she brings her own dinner. She even takes her own dinner to the White House. The only reason we inquired about the stove is in case some of hers has to be heated."

Around 6 P.M. the chauffeur-driven Cadillac limousine pulled up in front of our door (adding class to our neighborhood) and out stepped the Lowes. Carol, wearing a great Yves Saint Laurent sailor suit, looked smashing even with the large plastic insulated picnic basket she was carrying on her arm. When she walked through the door, she went immediately into the dining room and asked "Which is my chair?"

I showed her. She then placed her picnic dinner down beside *that* chair on the floor. Then we all went into the den for cocktails: tall glasses of cranberry juice—for everyone.

Carol and Charles are marvelous conversationalists, and we always have a lot to talk about. But I didn't pay too much attention to the conversation before dinner because one awful thought kept running through my mind. I kept thinking that maybe our standard poodle, Diva, might eat Carol's dinner on the floor before Carol got to it.

I'll never forget how our son (then fourteen) John's eyes widened as he watched Carol Channing poking around her picnic bag at dinner, coming up with a large Mason jar filled with pieces of some boiled dry meat.

Even as she scooped the meat out on to her plate, she managed to keep a running conversation going about current events and other things we were all interested in talking about. Another large jar she pulled out of her basket was filled to the brim with six or seven baked potatoes. These spuds had been organically grown and were baked in a special way. She ate at least three of these and was still slowly munching on her meat and potatoes throughout our dinner, even through the dessert. Charles, though, I remember, heartily enjoyed that soufflé.

One of us found it necessary to inquire just exactly what that "boiled out" meat was. Nonchalantly, Carol said, "It's moose meat." And her tone implied, "Doesn't everybody?"

After dinner we went back into the den to watch the superb television special of Arthur Miller's *Death of a Salesman*. Carol carried her picnic basket right along with her. And so help me, as you or I would eat popcorn while watching a show, Carol Channing munched on the remaining baked potatoes, popping bit by bit into her mouth, eating all the more vigorously as the tears came streaming down her face during the sadder moments of *Salesman*.

If Carol Channing's eating habits are a contributing factor to her great talent, then I suggest to other performers with far less talent that they start eating moose meat!

Carol and her husband are two of the hardest working people in show business. There's lots of kidding about Charles in the business, because he sometimes seems overzealous on behalf of his wife. But it would be a greatly needed service if he decided to open a school to teach theatrical management. He is superb in his job. Carol is lucky to have a man she can trust to handle not only her business but her personal life.

And Carol and Charles are loyal friends. Charles may ask for favors, but both he and Carol give as much as they get.

I happen to know of one instance where a newspaper friend of mine was for a brief (very brief) time without a job, when the paper she was with changed hands. The first person to call her when he thought she was jobless was Charles Lowe. He said, "If you need money or anything else, feel free to call upon us." She didn't need anything, but Charles had no way of knowing this. Not too many people know this about the Lowes, and I'm happy to be able to tell it. I hope I never need anything, but I think if I did, I too would be able to call on Charles Lowe and Carol Channing for help.

# A Dressing-down by
# the President of the United States

Around 9 P.M. we were leisurely dining on the terrace of the Carleton Hotel in Cannes, France, and gazing out at the brilliantly lit pride of the American Lines, the S.S. *Independence*.

At the table with us was honeymoon couple Mr. and Mrs. Dwight Hemion. Since then, Dwight Hemion has become a most important producer of TV specials, responsible for some wonderful Burt Bacharach, Barbra Streisand and Frank Sinatra shows.

The Dwight Hemions are now divorced.

All this is incidental to our story except what happened to me on board the S.S. *Independence* adds up to another of those most embarrassing moments.

At the time I was a young eager beaver NBC "Monitor" reporter. Well, the morning after we saw the ship anchored out at sea, I joined forces with 150 reporters from all over the continent to go out on a tender to the S.S. *Independence* to interview the President of the United States, Harry S. Truman.

Before the tender sailed, all the reporters were herded together on the dock and were given protocol instructions by the American FBI and also by the French Security Police.

I was the only member of the radio press there. And the only reporter who had a tape recorder.

Not too many of the others spoke English, so a delegation of multilingual fourth estaters came up to me and, in fractured French, asked if I would become the spokesman for the whole group. The plan was for me to record everything the President said on my tape recorder, including all the answers to the questions I would ask—for them.

I was plenty excited and thrilled about the fact that my voice would be the only one putting questions to the President of the United States.

As the tender approached the S.S. *Independence,* we saw hundreds of her passengers leaning over the side waving to no one in particular.

Sure enough, I recognized three faces up there—and they recognized me! The three faces I knew hanging over the railing belonged to composer Jule Styne, his then fiancée Madame Ruth Dubonnet and their friend, author Anita Loos. Just two weeks before we had been with Jule and Ruth in Rome. It was Jule Styne who wrote the Academy Award winning song "Three Coins in the Fountain." We waved frantically to each other. I couldn't wait to reach them to be able to brag that my mission this time had nothing to do with show business, but that I was about to interview the President of the United States!

Once on board, after briefly greeting my friends, I gave them the brush saying, with my nose up in the air, that I was sorry not to be able to spend more time with them but I was, after all, on my way to see Mr. Truman.

It wasn't necessary for me to elbow my way up to the front of the salon where President Truman would meet the press. My new non-English-speaking buddies cleared a path for me and ushered me right up to within a few feet from where Mr. Truman would stand when he arrived. They even made a place for my battery-operated tape recorder which, to them, other

than the President himself, was the most important
thing in the room.

In *he* walked. And up we all stood. Then brusquely
and very much to the point, the President said, "How
do you do, ladies and gentlemen. Let's get started because this ship has to move on."

The ship was on its way back to the States via a ten-
day cruise on the Mediterranean. After the conference Mr. Truman was to get off the ship in Cannes
and fly home to the States from Paris.

From the hundreds of questions handed to me by
the fourth-estate conglomerate, I asked the first question. Mr. Truman answered it. Then I asked ten more
in a row. He answered these. When I started to ask
still another he looked down at me (he was standing
and I was sitting right under his nose), shook his finger in my face and said, "Young lady, I am tired of
answering your questions. You are not the only reporter in this room. Don't you think it would be nice
if you let others have a chance?"

He frightened me so, I didn't dare speak up to say
that I was merely the spokesman for the group. Later
when I summoned up enough courage to explain, he
once again shook his finger at me and said, "That's
enough out of you. I don't want to hear another word
from you for the rest of this meeting."

I never uttered another word. One by one, in broken English, the reporters from France, Spain and
Italy began to ask their own questions. Just as President Truman was ready to call a halt to the press conference, he once again looked down on me and shook
his head as if to say, "I can't believe the whole thing."

Just as embarrassing as being scolded by the President of the United States was the fact that Jule Styne
and Ruth Dubonnet, whom I had snubbed earlier,
may have heard me being chastised by the President.
I hadn't realized that they had been standing in the
back of the salon and had caught my act which was
definitely a flop! All I could think of was "How can I

bribe them to keep their mouths shut when they get back to Sardi's?"

When we arrived back on shore, the newsmen gathered around my tape recorder and for three solid hours copied down all of President Truman's answers to the twelve questions I managed to get in before he chewed me out.

# More About Harry S. Truman

Several years ago I went to Kansas City to see Ginger Rogers perform in the play *Tovarich* at the Kansas City Star Theatre. Once there, I received an extra bonus.

Ginger, who was born in Independence, Missouri, was honored by a special "Ginger Rogers Day." Independence is just across the bridge from Kansas City. You can imagine how thrilled she was by the appearance next to her on the grandstand by Independence's most prominent citizen, former President of the United States, Harry S. Truman.

After all the public speeches and festivities were concluded, President Truman invited Ginger, her mother and me to go with him to see the Harry S. Truman Library.

There were guides enough to take us around, but Mr. Truman insisted on taking us himself from room to room, although he was guarded all the way by a Secret Service man.

When we reached the auditorium, Mr. Truman went up to the microphone and spoke a few words to show us just how good the sound system was. Still standing there, he insisted that Ginger and I try out our speaking voices over his prized amplifying system. Ginger's mother had a go at it too. Several times I literally pinched myself to make sure that it was I at that microphone with the man who will probably go down in history as one of the greatest Presidents of the United States.

Could this sweet gentle human being be the same irascible man who bawled me out, several years before, on board the S.S. *Independence?*

After the tour, he invited us to go back with him to his private office in the library, where each day he worked many long hours on the myriads of Truman speeches and manuscripts. He sat down behind his large desk and the three of us sat close by him in comfortable chairs.

Ginger's mother, Lela, talked with the President about an Independence they remembered from long ago. Ginger's recollections of Independence were not too clear, since her mother took her from there to live in Texas when Ginger was just a little girl.

President Truman sat at his desk talking with us about his wife, his daughter and his grandchildren, all of whom he was very proud.

We were there at the library with Mr. Truman for some three hours. When we noticed he was growing weary, Ginger got up and said she had to get back to the theatre.

The President insisted, "Before you go, let me see if I can find Bess. She'll be very angry with me if I tell her that Ginger Rogers was here and we didn't bring her over to meet you!"

Mr. Truman then asked his secretary to call Mrs. Truman at home. After trying to reach her, the secretary told the President that Mrs. Truman was out. Mr. Truman said, "I bet I know where she is. She went fishing today. Bess loves to go fishing." There was something warm and "for real" about this man sitting there talking about his family. It was difficult to equate this same person with the one (one of the few) who

144

had the guts to make any and every important decision when he was President of the United States!

Harry S. Truman himself escorted us out to the car which was waiting to take us back to Kansas City.

Before we drove off, I asked him if he would send me an autographed picture. The Secret Service man took down my address and Ginger's because she too asked for one. Two weeks later an autographed picture of former President Truman arrived at our house. I immediately put it in a silver frame on the piano, where it stands today.

Ginger Rogers and her mother, both Republicans, had the same goose bumps I did from spending time with Harry S. Truman, the *MAN*.

Last December, when former President Truman died, I sat and remembered the warmth and humility of this truly great statesman.

# Interview with B.B. Bardot

In 1958, on our first trip to Europe, Paris naturally was an important port of call. Brigitte Bardot was, at that time, one of the hottest movie names—more so in America than in France.

All through Europe I heard various media reporters complaining because none of them had been able to obtain interviews with the French "sex kitten."

When we arrived in Paris, I tried over and over again, going through proper channels, to get to her for NBC "Monitor." The only response I got was, "Sorrée, Miss Bardot is bissée making the film. And when she is making the film she see no one!"

Columnist Earl Wilson was staying at the George V Hotel, as we were, and he too had been trying for several weeks to get to La Bardot, without luck.

A couple of days before it was time for us to leave Paris, I met Eddie Constantine, an American actor who was making it "big" in French films. As a matter of fact, at the time he was one of Europe's highest paid movie stars. I told him about the difficulties I was having getting to Miss B.B. (pronounced Bébé). Constantine said he would try to help. He apparently knew her well. Just a few years before, B.B. had a small part in a picture in which Eddie had been the star. He said he couldn't promise me an interview, but if I would go with him to the studio the next day he might be able to at least introduce me to her.

"B.-Day" arrived! Movie stars in Paris do not start working until after lunch. There is no 7 A.M. call as there is in Hollywood. Directors in Paris claim that dispositions and faces are better in the afternoon than they are in the morning. American female movie stars agree with the French theory, but cannot convince the American producers of its validity.

At two o'clock on the dot, actor Constantine carried me off in his French sports car to a studio near Versailles.

When we arrived, we were told that Bardot was upstairs in her dressing room talking on the telephone to New York. A *Life* photographer, pacing up and down in front of the staircase, spotted my tape recorder and mumbled, "You'll never get her to talk on that. I've been hanging around here on assignment for weeks. She hasn't yet posed for one picture. Any shots I've gotten, I've had to sneak. All that dame keeps saying is, 'I'm not in the mood to pose.' I hope she comes to America where maybe she can be taught manners!"

A little later a *Newsweek* reporter said to Eddie, "Tell your friend there [meaning me] she is wasting her time. Brigitte just turned us down for a cover photo."

At that very moment B.B.'s secretary came down the stairs, saying to Constantine, "If you wait a while, she will see you." Eddie was so busy being interviewed by reporters himself, he didn't notice that time was running out—my time!

After a while, Eddie Constantine told me, "I don't think she's going to see me or you. Let's go back to your hotel."

We were about to leave, much to the amusement of *Life* and *Newsweek* who were still standing around in the wings, when that famous sexy voice belonging to B.B. called from the top of the stairs, "Eddieeee, come on up."

He dashed up the stairs. Then her secretary called down to me and said, *"Vous aussi,"* which means "you too."

In high school French I asked if I could bring my tape recorder up with me. "But, of course," she replied.

Well, did I ever walk by *Life* and *Newsweek* with my nose up in the air!

There, in a chair in front of the dressing-table mirror, making up, sat a beautiful child-woman, who turned and held out her hand saying, "I am delighted to see you."

I don't know what powers of persuasion my pal Constantine had used, but he must have known Groucho's secret "woid."

"Miss Bardot," I began, "you are probably one of the most important stars in the U.S.A. today. Do you have any idea of how popular you are in the States?"

Brigitte replied, "Please call me Brigitte. Yes, some friends recently returned from your countreee and told me. I am verree pleased!"

Brigitte Bardot was everything in person that she was on screen. Plenty sexy. Raquel Welch on screen today is somewhat like her, except Brigitte seemed to have qualities of naiveté and humility which are attributes Miss Welch definitely does not have, at least for me. Brigitte seemed all-knowing and ten years old at the same time. She spoke English very well, although she didn't think so. She said she learned the language from the English-speaking reporters.

I remember asking her if she had the desire to wear pretty clothes in pictures like those worn by America's Joan Crawford or Lana Turner. "No," she replied. "How you say, *les moines possible* [the less possible], too much clothes is heavy to my boddee."

Brigitte Bardot also said that she never went to a

hairdresser. She cannot stand to have anyone touch her hair. "Also, I nevaire wear a hat. I have hair to cover my head. That is enough, no?"

At this point my tape recorder broke down and I thought for sure she would throw me out. After all, *Life* had to sneak their pictures, and she wouldn't even pose for the cover of *Newsweek*. Believe it or not, she smiled and told me to take my time fixing the machine. "If necessaire, we will do it all over again, yes?"

As a matter of fact, Eddie Constantine and B.B. Bardot helped fix the machine. Then we continued with the interview.

She told me, "I would love to do a film with Frankeee Sinatra [bet at the time Frankee would have loved doing a picture with B.B.]. I would love to come to your countree, America—and make the movie. But, alas, I have a contract to stay here. It is my fondest dream to come to America. I would like some peace and quiet for a change!"

Peace and quiet in the United States? I thought, "You poor deluded girl!"

Brigitte continued by talking about her acting. "My acting is different now. But, *comment vous dit?*" she asked of Eddie Constantine. "How you say, the character I play is the same girl as in *God Created Woman* but I play it more better now."

At this point the director sent word that they were ready for her. "Come downstairs with Eddiee and watch me work, no?" I explained that I would like to have a picture taken with her. She said we would have one taken after the scene.

We went down to the set together, past *Life*, past *Newsweek* and past a slew of other reporters.

I watched her shoot a love scene in which she had to kiss her leading man (who resembled a road-company John Boles) over and over again through a chiffon veil! Often it is boring to watch a movie in the making, but this was fascinating. How often do you watch people kissing through veils?

Eddie Constantine wasn't exactly thrilled to be standing around for that extra hour. Could be, he had been there before with B.B., both on and off screen. Something had given him his "special" influence.

Hours later (at least it seemed like hours later), when Brigitte finished the scene, I went up to her with a large smile. Hadn't we become buddies up in her dressing room? I said, "Now, Brigitte, can we have that picture together?"

She looked through me as if she had never seen me before. "I am sorree," she said. "No pictures, now. I am not in ze mood." And up the stairs she went to her dressing room.

I was utterly fascinated by her change of moods. I had no cause to complain—I had gotten a hell of a good interview with Brigitte Bardot and was delighted to be one of a very select group of reporters who, at the time, had been able to get to her at all.

Although Miss Bardot is no longer the hot box-office attraction she was then, I'm told she is still a difficult interview to obtain. Well, once is "more better," as she might say, "than nevaire."

# Look Ma, I'm a Movie Star

"How would you like a part in the movie *Palm Springs Weekend?*" asked Warner Brothers publicist Dorothy Atlas on the long-distance horn from L.A. Every female would like to be in a movie, at least once in her lifetime, if only for laughs.

"You mean," I asked, "I'd have a speaking part?" Dorothy assured me that Warner Brothers had agreed to give me lines. This was in September. "How soon do I have to be out in Hollywood?" Press agent Atlas said the movie was set to go into production soon, and for me to stand by.

So I stood by all of September, October and November. By December first, I decided to call Dorothy at Warner Brothers. I was sure by now the picture was already completed, and I hadn't heard from her because she was afraid to break the news to me.

I forgot to mention that for a good part of September and October I kept reporting in my column that any day now I would be on my way to Hollywood as an actress, yet!

Dorothy explained that the picture had been postponed until February. How could she have known that my bags had been packed since September? When I told her about the bulging suitcases, she apologized and said someone should have notified me.

Well, neither the picture nor I had been canceled. And February wasn't so far off.

In February, I read in our own Detroit *Free Press* that Warner Brothers had started production on *Palm Springs Weekend*. And that the story dealt with Palm Springs at Eastertime, when the thousands of the college kids descended upon the place.

Once again, at my own expense, I called the Warner Brothers publicity office in Burbank and told them what I had read in the newspaper. Was it true? It was! The picture was already filming, but they were not ready for me yet. I was to sit tight in Detroit and wait for their call. I sat so tight in Detroit I turned down two movie junkets, one to Paris and one to London. I knew Europe would always be there, but when would I get a second chance to be in a Hollywood movie?

February went by with no call for me from the studio. Since my children, Toni and John, were on vacation from Grosse Pointe University School, I talked my husband into taking them and me to Beverly Hills for their ten-day hiatus from doing whatever it was they did in school, although this year we had not planned a family Easter trip. I figured if I was somewhere on the Hollywood scene, just in case Warners had decided not to use me, seeing me around might shame them into keeping their commitment.

One day, two days, five days, nine days of the kids' vacation passed by, and it was almost time for us to go home.

On the ninth day I again called Warner Brothers. Now I was really angry at them—and at myself for having been duped into thinking I was going to be in a movie.

My husband was plenty upset since it had cost him several thousand bucks to bring the kids to the Beverly Hills Hotel so they could watch Mama working in a picture with such stars as Troy Donahue, Connie Francis, Stefanie Powers and that really big star Ty Hardin. And my normally patient, quiet husband became pretty vocal about it. This prompted me to call Dorothy Atlas and shout: "I'm going home tomorrow."

She asked if I could stay on a few more days because my part had just been written. She had seen the script and she was sure they would be needing me momentarily.

Since I had paid, or rather Edward had paid, my plane fare out, if I went home to Detroit and had to be brought back, Warners would then have to send me the fare.

This put the studio into immediate action. That same evening, delivered by special messenger, came the script—or at least my part. It arrived at the hotel along with a note saying to stand by for an immediate call. This meant I would be going to work at last!

When I showed Edward the three blue pages of script, he said, "You're not really going to stick around for this, are you?"

Of course I was. After all, I wasn't about to let a whole studio down. Things were bad enough in the motion-picture business. Who was I to add to the industry's woes!!

My husband and children went home. I stayed on. Fortunately, Edward did not really read the three blue pages. If he had, he would have noticed that on those pages only three of the lines belonged to me.

Over a period of years, staying at the Beverly Hills Hotel, often I would hear actors and actresses coming home in the evening from the studios, tell Leon, the doorman, to have their cars waiting at 5 A.M. the next morning because they had a six o'clock studio call. Well, soon it would be my turn to say it!

Now, with script in hand, I was determined that when the time came, I would not only know my lines, I would say them with *feeling!* Soooo I went to Ginger Rogers' house to get her interpretation of how to play the part. She actually took the time to go over it with me.

I asked Barbara Stanwyck for help, but she said, "You're on your own, kid. My advice to you is to go home to your husband and children."

Kathryn Grayson hummed the lines. Happily for Bette Davis, she was in Connecticut; and luckily for Joan Crawford, she was in New York.

By the time I got the call from Warners to show up for work, at least a dozen friends in the business knew the lines better than I did.

A fourth assistant to director Norman Taurog called to say that I should be at the studio and in makeup by 8 the next morning. At 5 P.M. that same evening I gave Leon, the doorman, the little speech I had been waiting so long to recite.

"Leon," I said, "have my car ready at 5 A.M. I have an early morning call at the studio!"

Then I went up to my room and called down for room service. Although Barbara Stanwyck wouldn't help me with the part, she did say "You must go to bed early so you don't have bags under your eyes on camera when you go to work tomorrow."

It was only six in the evening, but having already had my bath and dinner, I got into bed and read and reread, spoke and respoke those three lousy lines. It was still daylight so I pulled the shades down and the curtains across the window to darken the room. Then I told the operator to be sure to call me at four-thirty the next morning.

I tried to sleep but couldn't. I tossed and I turned, and I worried. At ten o'clock I wanted to throw up, but was afraid it might cause lines around my mouth, so with much mind over matter, I managed not to. Twelve o'clock, one o'clock, two o'clock, and I still couldn't fall asleep. By the time the operator rang with the four-thirty wake-up call, I was fully dressed and ready to go out to the studio in Burbank.

At five o'clock, I picked up the keys to my car at

the front desk because at that hour of the morning there was no attendant at the door. Then off I went to Warner Brothers arriving at the studio only fifteen minutes later, because there was no traffic.

A sleepy night watchman stopped me from driving through the gates onto the lot. He demanded to know what my business was. I explained that my business was to be an actress this day in a film called *Palm Springs Weekend*. I gave him my name. He took forever to peruse a long sheet of names. Finally he said, "Yeah, you're expected all right, but not until eight o'clock."

Since it was only five-fifteen, I didn't know what else to do except to ask if it was all right for me to wait outside the makeup building. "I guess so," he said gruffly. "Although I don't think there will be anyone in there for a long while."

After giving instructions on how to find the makeup building, he let me drive through.

I kept thinking, as I drove onto the deserted lot, "Here I am driving at the same studio where before me Errol Flynn, Bette Davis, Olivia De Havilland, Jimmy Cagney, Bogart, Stanwyck, etc., etc. all had worked. What a kick this whole adventure was.

I parked my car in front of makeup and some fifteen minutes later several people in the department began to arrive. Not knowing what else to do, they put me in a chair in a makeup room and kept bringing me cups of black coffee. Finally, about seven-thirty, Fred Williams, the man who was to make me up, came in, took a look and said, "You must have been up late last night. Don't worry, we'll hide those rings under your eyes."

Now the place was bustling. Natalie Wood was being made up in the next booth, and that gave me a kind of glow in spite of the fact that she would be coming out of her booth looking a hell of a lot better than I would. But she had points on me going in!

When Fred finished his Pygmalion-like feat of glamorizing this reporter, a lady came in to do the body makeup. No, my scene was not in the nude! Had it been a horror film they may have so used me. Body makeup meant my arms and hands, since I was to wear a sleeveless dress—one of my own, incidentally, because a three-line part did not warrant a special dress from wardrobe. You see, unless it's a period film, extras and bit players must furnish their own clothes.

Came the time to walk over to the set. When I arrived on the sound stage where *Palm Springs Weekend* was shooting, I was flabbergasted to see, in the long line of portable dressing rooms, one with the name "SHIRLEY EDER" posted on it. It was situated between Connie Stevens and Troy Donahue. Like WOW! They were really giving me the special A-1 treatment.

I walked into a flower-filled dressing room, just like actresses do in the movies! There was one vase filled with posies sent by Mary Martin and Richard Halliday. Another from Anne Jeffreys and Robert Sterling. Still another from Ginger Rogers. And on the makeup table were dozens of telegrams all wishing me luck. Maybe my being in this movie was just for fun, but after seeing all those flowers and receiving some of the "star" treatment, I felt like "Queen for a Day."

Off in a corner I saw about four dozen American Beauty roses wrapped in wrinkled green wax paper tied together with a red ribbon. I thought some florist had nerve using crummy old wax paper. The enclosed card read "A star is born. Good luck and love, Hugh Benson." Hugh, at the time, headed the Warner Brothers TV department. A still cameraman came in and took a picture of me holding those roses in my arms.

Director Norman Taurog asked that all members of the cast please assemble onstage. Suddenly, I was so scared I wanted to lock myself inside the dressing room. However, the real me, which is 1,000 per cent ham, saw to it that I went out onto the set with the others.

"Ladies and gentlemen," said Mr. Taurog (this is the same Norman Taurog whose name Howard Hughes falsely used when we spoke that one time on the phone), "I have a telegram here I would like to read aloud. It says, 'Dear Norman, this morning you have a new actress on your hands. Shirley Eder. I happen to know she is difficult to get along with and very temperamental. I want to assure you that if she gives you too much trouble, as a favor to you, I'm available for her part. Much love,' and it is signed 'Barbara Stanwyck.' "

Taurog read it straight and then burst out laughing.

Waiting in the wings, so to speak, to do my part, I went around interviewing the various stars in the film, so it shouldn't be a total loss.

And then I heard it! I heard my name being called by Mr. Taurog's first assistant. It was time to go into my scene which took place in a record shop in Palm Springs. Stefanie Powers, behind a counter, was to sell me a record saying, "Here you are, Miss Eder. I hope you play it on your TV show."

Would you believe my only three lines were "Thank you, dear" (line one), "Oh" (line two), "Please remember me to your father" (line three). Between the "Thank you, dear" and the "Oh," I was to open my pocketbook, take out some money and hand it over to Stefanie. Then, I was to turn and walk part of the way out of the shop and say, "Please remember me to your father" just as I saw Troy Donahue coming into the shop.

Wanting to show how clever and letter-perfect I was, I did the whole bit in thirty seconds. Mr. Taurog came up, patted my face and said, "That was fine. Now let's try it again. This time much slower. That way, you see, you'll be on screen for a longer period of time."

Back I went in front of the counter, behind which Miss Powers was still standing. I'll never forget how she whispered before the cameras rolled for the second take, "Fumble around a lot in your pocketbook looking for the money. That way they'll keep the camera on you a whole lot longer."

I fumbled like crazy, this time because I couldn't really find the phony money I had been handed before we started. It had somehow slipped out onto the floor. Naturally, this meant doing the scene over for a third time.

Several days earlier when I first met Mr. Taurog, I remember saying to him kiddingly, "You will give me a close-up, won't you?"

Sure enough, at the end of take three, somebody came up with a long tape measure, stuck it on the tip of my nose and walked back several paces. So help me, I thought they were just measuring my nose. What they were doing was lining up the camera angles for the close-up.

It took some thirty minutes for them to break down whatever it is they have to break down to rearrange the cameras and equipment to set up for a close-up.

Could I dare tell Mr. Taurog not to shoot my profile? Left or right, my profile doesn't exactly resemble Elizabeth Taylor's. I was afraid my nose was too big for such intimacy with a camera. Of course, this was before Barbra Streisand made noses the "in" thing!

Finally, just before lunch break, my scene was wrapped and in the can. (That's movie talk for its being finished.) And my footage just might have ended up in a different kind of can.

Still in the key light, walking out of the scene, I heard applause. I should say applau' because it was only one person clapping. My friends Mitzi Gaynor and Florence Brachman had been sitting in director's chairs watching the close-up bit. It was Mitzi who applauded. Two days earlier the girls had promised to show up to lend me moral support. I had forgotten all about it, but apparently they hadn't. Had I known that Mitzi Gaynor was sitting out there watching, I probably would have frozen with stage fright.

Mitzi and Florence took me to the famous Green Room in the Warner commissary for lunch. After lunch they helped carry all the flowers from the dressing room to the car.

It was a little embarrassing walking past the grips and stagehands with those many flowers sent for just three lousy lines. But it was a hell of a lot more embarrassing when, while carrying the American Beauty roses wrapped in the wrinkled green wax paper with the red ribbon still on it, we reached the car and the prop man came running after me saying, "Where do you think you are going with those roses?"

I told him I was taking them home with the rest of the flowers.

"You can't take those out of the studio. They belong to the prop department." I felt the roses. Sure enough, they were made of wax!

Hugh Benson, who sent them, figured I would know they were phony, all wrapped in green paper with the red ribbon. But I was so carried away by the movie debut, I never once suspected it was a gag.

I received one hundred dollars for the day's work with many deductions, of course, taken from the check including the standard 1 per cent for the benefit of the motion-picture home.

Several years later, *Palm Springs Weekend* was sold to television and I couldn't believe it when I received a residual check for seventy-five dollars. Eight months after that another one came in for forty dollars. Just last week, after I don't know how many showings of the movie on television, I received what is probably the final residual check. The Screen Actors Guild sent me $1.60.

It took about ten years to get invited to do another movie. I was given five lines in *C.C. and Company,* starring Ann-Margret and Joe Namath. This time, instead of waiting at my own expense to do the job, I showed up on location in Arizona the same day and left for home that evening. What's more, *C.C. and*

*Company* paid my plane fare there and back. Nobody was going to make a sucker out of me twice—no siree.

So how come I still have never been paid for the day's work in *C.C. and Company?*

# A Ride With John Glenn

Via this book, I am breaking the news to my husband and my other love, Cary Grant, that there is yet another man in my life! With this man I would fly to the moon—*literally*. His name is John Glenn!

We were up in Atlanta, Michigan, where Edward Cole, president of General Motors, owns a heap big parcel of farm land. Dollie Cole gave a surprise birthday party for her husband, and we were among the invited guests.

While some of the others were fishing or hitting golf balls or feeding the llama (yep, they have one) or eating freshly picked corn, I decided to take a ride on one of those tiny-trail Hondas.

For some reason I couldn't get the dang thing started. John Glenn, another guest, came over and fooled around with the baby Honda for me, but he couldn't get it started either. It was a little disappointing to hear John Glenn, the first Yank to go around the world in space, say, "I don't know the first thing about mini bikes." But to his credit at least he does tell the truth. He really didn't know anything about mini bikes. Finally Edward Cole, the Master Mechanic, came over to the bike, got under it with an oil can, pulled a little gadget, and I was on my way. It took the president of the largest corporation in the world to know that all it needed was a spritz of oil.

Up—up and away I flew. Several miles from the main house, but still on Cole land, the tiny bike sputtered, gasped, then dropped dead. Fortunately for me, Joseph, the Coles' fifteen-year-old son, came by with a pal and said the machine had simply run out of gas. The boys took the thing from me, attaching it to their larger bike, went on and left me standing there. Obviously they forgot about me, and I became a little panicky after about a half hour. This was only August, but I had visions of being left out there in the wilderness through the winter snows and not being discovered until the spring thaw. I'm talking, naturally, about my body being found. Then along came "my hero" on a big noisy motorcycle. As he whizzed by I yelled, "Help. I'm lost!" My hero was John Glenn.

He turned around, came back and made some inane remark about "What are you doing way out here without a vehicle?" Then in astro-knightly fashion he shouted: "Hop on!"

Shouting into the wind as we roared homeward, me sitting behind him with my arms wound tightly around his waist, "I feel so safe with you at the wheel, John!"

He called back, "I'm glad you feel that way, but I don't know how safe you are. I'm kind of new at motorcycling. I never drove one before!" This didn't exactly give me even false courage. But, by golly, we arrived back at the house without mishap. Would you believe that I wasn't missed by anyone, including my husband? Hadn't anyone realized that if Glenn hadn't rescued me, maybe I would never have been found at all?

I have met many of the other astronauts and their wives on various visits to Houston. They are all very nice men, especially bachelor Al Werdon, who is the cutest. But John and his wife, Annie, are special. They are warm and gracious people. John is extremely modest and has the kind of humility one rarely finds in a public hero.

That day on the Cole farm he and I spoke seriously of the space program. I asked whether he thought all future flights into space should be halted. Glenn said that because there were things on earth which were needed more we should cut back, but not too far back. "If we stop completely," he said, "and have to start all over again at some future date, it will cost the government that much more money to build whole new crafts and teams. It is definitely important to the United States to set up space stations. If we call a halt to the entire program, we won't set them up." He told me this in 1970.

I asked him how long it would take to get to Mars. He figured, with the knowhow we had at that time, it would take about two years to get there and back.

Did he want to go to the moon? Did he ever! But he knew he would never have the chance to do so. He was too old, now.

What did John Glenn think about on *that* day waiting in the spacecraft, as the very first man to orbit the world? He said he was too busy to think about anything except what he was doing. Then he laughed and said, "You know, what you really think about once everything is in order? You think—here you are, sitting on top of something made for the government by the very *lowest* bidder."

Meeting John Glenn, American astronaut, was a thrill. Meeting John Glenn, the man, was pure joy.

# An Evening with
# Hugh O'Brian and—?

Hugh O'Brian, who was starring in *Cactus Flower* at the Fisher Theatre in Detroit, went to supper with us at Topinka's, a restaurant across the street from the theatre. His date that night was a darling young (and I mean *very* young) actress who had come in from New York over the weekend to see him. At the time, she was working as a dancer in a show in New York.

I remember the four of us sitting in a booth, with me next to Hugh on one side, and his girl between Hugh and my husband. Hugh spent most of the evening talking to me. She, in turn, spent the evening talking to Edward, who found her adorable (and she was). Mind you, all the while Hugh was talking to me and she was talking to Edward—she and Hugh held hands.

It wasn't that Mr. O'Brian was so fascinated by me or my conversation. It was that he has never been adverse to publicity, and I do happen to write a column. Admittedly, I was not adverse to having Mr. O'Brian so attentive to me. Hugh is a knowledgeable and entertaining man.

Very *sotto voce*, because I didn't want to hurt the feelings of his date, I asked him questions about his recently finished affair (if it was that) with Princess Soraya. From what I had heard and from what he was now saying, he and Soraya had definitely had a romance. But whatever was between them once was now finito. I don't think he addressed more than ten sentences the entire evening to his young date. I'm sure he noticed that she was being well taken care of by my husband.

At one point Hugh whispered that he really was crazy about the kid and he was seriously considering marrying her. Lots of years have gone by since then and Mr. O'Brian did not marry her nor has he married anyone else. Obviously, marriage is not his bag.

I paid no real attention to her name when we were introduced. On the way home, in the car with Edward, I asked if he knew the name of Hugh's cute date. He said he caught her first name but not her last.

Since that night, we often bump into Hugh, in Hollywood and other places. I even played poker at his Beverly Hills home. I like Hugh O'Brian. He works hard at his craft, which means beside the actual acting part, he is always available for interviews. Many of his peers scoff at his ready availability to the press, but whether they admit it or not, it has paid off for him.

One day recently I received a long-distance call from Hugh O'Brian asking me to try and catch a TV show called "Probe" in which he was starring. Actually, it was a pilot for a show which subsequently did go on the air as a series. I don't know what made me ask him that day if he ever saw the cute kid he had brought to supper with us several years before in Detroit. I reminded him that he had said, "This is the one girl I'd like to marry."

"I can't remember her name, Hugh, but whatever happened to her?"

"You're putting me on," he exclaimed. "You certainly must know about her."

It took me a few minutes to convince him that I

really wasn't "putting him on." I couldn't remember her name, because I never knew it.

"Well," he continued, "that little girl, whom I really thought I'd like to marry, is now a bright young star and is doing just fine. Her name is Sandy Duncan!"

I thought then that he was "putting me on." He wasn't! It was absolutely true that Hugh O'Brian, Sandy Duncan, Edward and I had all supped together, that night in Detroit.

When I told my husband who Hugh's date had been, he said, "You know, every time I see that girl on television in a commercial or on her own show I have the feeling that I know her from someplace!"

At the time Hugh called about "Probe," Sandy was recovering from her serious eye operation. Although she had married someone else since Detroit and was in the process of a divorce, Hugh visited Sandy in the hospital every day he was permitted to see her. They have remained good friends.

At the 1972 Academy Award ball I went over to Sandy's table, introduced myself and reminded her that we had actually met years before in Detroit. She didn't remember my name either, but she did recall the night and how very nice my husband had been to her while Hugh spent most of the time talking to me.

Sandy Duncan was delightful before she became famous and was just darling that night at the Oscar ball. People don't change. Success just makes them more of what they really are.

Betcha Raquel Welch was exactly the same as a teen-ager, as she is now, only now she is *more so— uggh!*

# Mystery Guest

I remember one summer, not too long ago, when people of affluence in our community were giving oneupmanship parties. You know the kind I mean. Someone would take over the ballroom at the big Pontchartrain Hotel and hire a thirty-piece band. Then another would hire a twenty-piece band with an extra twenty-piece orchestra to play while the first rested. Others brought in superstars to sing and be funny, at the "club date" going rates, i.e., $3,500 a shot.

Then, smaller more select gatherings began to take the place of the larger soirees with mystery guests as the bait to best each other. For instance, I went to one party where everyone invited had to bring along a surprise guest. Someone brought the city's leading disc jockey. Another brought the then top baseball player of the Detroit Tigers, Denny McLain. These parties went on for one whole year—then somehow they were phased out.

One day during that summer I received a call from the public relations director of Bantam Books, Esther Margolis, saying that she was coming through town with a famous author who had written a hardback

best seller which was now being published in paper-
back. They were coming in on a weekend.

Although Esther knew that newspaper people dis-
liked working on Saturdays, she asked if I minded
doing an interview on Saturday or on Sunday with
her author.

Saturday for me was out of the question because of
previous plans, but Sunday was fine. I definitely
wanted to meet and speak with *this* author. I asked
them to come to my house in the afternoon because
we were going to someone's home for dinner.

Miss Margolis and her author arrived. I was not
only fascinated by what the author had to say, I
genuinely liked her. Discovering that they had no
other appointments until Monday morning and knowing that there were very few restaurants open on
Sunday nights, I thought they might enjoy coming to
our friends' house for dinner. Of course, I called the
hostess to see if it was all right. It was not only all
right, she was thrilled to have this particular celebrity
in her home. She asked me, however, not to tell anyone about it beforehand, because she wanted to make
the author *the* mystery guest of the month.

The hostess asked if I would stop and pick up a
neighbor who was also coming to dinner, because this
woman's husband was playing golf at the country
club. This way they wouldn't have to drive home that
night in two cars. Incidentally, our hosts lived on the
grounds of the country club.

Well, I called my neighbor Bea to tell her what
time we would pick her up and asked if she minded
showing the visitors her home and art collection. Bea
has a nationwide reputation for owning one of the
best collections of kinetic art. Neighbor Bea asked the
name of the author. I explained that until we arrived
at her house it would have to remain a mystery.

She asked, "Is it a man?" I wouldn't answer that.
"Well, then," she exclaimed, "it has to be a woman,"
and then began enumerating the current female authors.

"I can't say yes," I explained, "and I can't say no but you'll see for yourself soon enough."

The three of us got out of the car in front of Bea's house, rang the bell, and as soon as she opened the door I said, "Bea I want you to meet Esther Margolis and Christine Jorgensen."

"Oh, my God! You're kidding!" exclaimed Bea in a state of shock. "No, you're not kidding. It is—oh yes it is, I've seen you on television." Christine just laughed and explained that she was used to people greeting her in this manner. When we went through the house, it was evident that Christine knew a great deal about art.

It was still too early to go to the party, so we went to the country club first for a drink. The weather was bleak, so there weren't too many people hanging around the clubhouse. As soon as we arrived, Bea excused herself, saying she'd be right back.

Christine Jorgensen said, "You know what she is doing, don't you? She's rounding up all her friends to come and have a look at me." This amused Chris, especially when a few moments later people seemed to be coming out of the woodwork. You could see them peeking in from outside the clubhouse window, while others came and sat near us on the patio.

Some less timid members came up to the table and introduced themselves, still gaping. Christine was charming and appeared interested in all their nonsensical small talk. She was used to it. Need I say that they were very definitely interested in her.

We drove around the club grounds to our hostess' house. She greeted us at the door in a most nonchalant way, as if Christine Jorgensen showed up there for dinner every night. She could have won an Oscar for her cool performance.

We walked into the room where the other guests were gathered. No one paid attention to our entrance until the hostess in a nervous voice introduced Esther Margolis and Christine Jorgensen. The room suddenly grew quiet. If you were a collector of eyeballs, you would have had a bonanza, picking them all up from the floor as they fell. The host grabbed me by the arm, whispering, "Jesus Christ! Why didn't you give me some warning?"

My own husband, who hadn't known about the interview, arrived moments after we did, looked at me as if to say, "How could you do this?" He has learned to expect the unexpected, having been married to me for so many years, but this time he was thrown into a state of shock!

Among the guests there were a doctor and his wife. Before long the doctor and Chris were discussing her famous operation. She had no qualms about discussing it. After all, she had written a best-selling book telling the whole story.

Pretty soon, people began to gravitate toward her. Many sat on the floor at her feet. All the earlier titters and snide innuendoes were now forgotten. Everybody became genuinely interested in Christine as a human being instead of as an oddity. The clinical talk between the doctor and Christine Jorgensen was fascinating, and no one in the room wanted to miss a word.

By the time dinner was over, and we were all on our way into the projection room to see a movie, Chris had become just another guest.

Christine Jorgensen is a bright interesting woman, who for a period of time lived through hell. She was able to overcome her deep unhappiness and emerge as a happy respected citizen. Also her guts in telling the story in print has helped many people with the same problem all over the world.

On December 1, 1952, Christine Jorgensen underwent the first transsexual surgery and changed from George W. Jorgensen, Jr., former GI, into a lovely woman named Christine. Because of her frankness and courage, that same operation is now performed regularly without fanfare or publicity for either the doctors or the patients.

# Greater Love Hath No Husband

"Please help me carry this tape recorder," I asked my husband as we were leaving the Beverly Hills Hotel to go to Malibu Beach to do an interview with Lana Turner, and to have dinner with her afterward.

"Cook," (short for the endearment word "Cookie") replied Edward, "you know I hurt my back on the diving board this morning. I can't carry anything." So I carried the fifteen-pound machine. I was used to it, anyway. On the way to Malibu in the car I kept nagging Edward, in typical wifely fashion, saying how fat he was getting and that he should do more exercise and that he should eat less. Harp, harp, harp all the way to Lana Turner's house.

Lana lived in the chic part of Malibu, known as the "Colony." Her female secretary (now she has a handsome male) opened the door and brought us right to the bar saying, "L.T." would be down in a moment. That moment stretched to forty-five minutes. But it was well worth the forty-five minute wait, especially for Edward whose eyes bugged out of his head watching Lana make her entrance, wafting down the stairs to the bar wearing a seductive mumu. Immediately, she put her arms around my husband's corpulent middle, saying, "Eduardo, you look divine. You've taken off so much weight." With her arms still about him, he turned to give me a snotty look, which in husband-wife lingo meant "See, only you think I'm getting fat."

"Eduardo," who never ever drinks martinis, guzzled a grown man's share of them that night as did our hostess. Sipping a ginger ale, I stood off to one side making small talk with the secretary. By now it was evening, and though we were invited for dinner, my nose told me there was nothing cooking. I shouldn't say that because actually there was something cooking—Eduardo and Lana! Eventually, Lana said, "My cook is out, so I made us a reservation at a little restaurant down the beach."

Into the car we piled, Eduardo and Lana in the front seat, Shirley and the secretary in the back. It didn't matter since it was a very short ride to the restaurant.

We sat in a booth in this three-fourths empty restaurant and ordered dinner. I distinctly remember Edward ordering a lobster first, then steak, baked potato, salad and a vegetable.

There was a dance floor with no one dancing on it. The music was being piped in from Muzak. Lana ordered a minimum amount of food and a maximum amount of martinis. Her secretary, too, was on a martini kick. I was on my seventh glass of ginger ale when Lana said, "Edward, come dance with me." There was nothing unusual about this request—except . . . For openers Edward Slotkin is an ultraconservative type fella who would never get up on a dance floor unless there were other couples on it. You can imagine my surprise when he jumped to his feet, took the luscious Lana by her hand and led her onto the empty dance floor where they danced to Muzak, yet!

They danced through his lobster and through his steak, potato, vegetable and salad too. Now I was concerned! The fact that he was still half of the only couple on the floor after an hour was indicative of something. But more important was the fact that Edward, who would rather eat than do anything in the whole wide world (and I do mean *anything*), never came back to the table to even taste his food. What's more, Lana's secretary mumbled, "If I were you, I'd take him home."

It was warm in that restaurant. But on the dance floor, the sweat that was pouring from my husband's face wasn't all from the heat in the room!

At last they came back to the table. Edward, not touching his food, went to the men's room. Was he looking for a cold shower? Lana, ignoring her food for another martini, pointed a finger at me, and said jokingly (I think), "If I wanted to, I could take Edward away from you just like that." She snapped her fingers. Not knowing what else to do, I laughed. "Don't laugh," continued one of the most glamorous women in the whole wide world. "I mean," she smiled, still joking (I think), "I could take him away from you for all time."

Up until then I had been really amused by the marvelous time my newly uninhibited old husband had been having.

Now, somewhere inside of me, a warning signal flashed this message: "Shirley, it's time to go home." And the slurred voice of the secretary mumbled, "I told you, I told you!"

The one thing that made me really mad was because Edward's back hurt he couldn't possibly carry the fifteen-pound tape recorder, but somehow he was able, for one hour straight, to dream up dance steps that could make Gower Champion take a back seat.

While Edward was still in the men's room, a handsome, but swarthy-looking young man came from across the room and introduced himself to Miss Turner. She was interested—thank God! When Edward returned to the table, sweatless but looking haggard, I suggested it was time to go home. He happily agreed, and so did Lana. Thank heaven for that young man who possibly reminded L.T. that Edward maybe wasn't as attractive as she had thought earlier.

The four of us went back to the car. Me—up front with my old man, and this time, Lana and the secretary in the back seat.

After depositing the girls at Lana's posh pad, we silently drove back to Beverly Hills. When we got to the hotel, I handed Edward the tape recorder, which had not even been used during the evening. And do you know he had the nerve to say, "Cook, you know my back is killing me!" When we got up to our rooms he said, "No greater love hath any husband than I have for my wife—I came home with *you* tonight." Then he laughed and I laughed too. That gorgeous woman Lana Turner (and she is) might have been able to borrow my husband for a night, but I knew for sure she never could have him for all time (I think)!

# Temper, Temper

Prominent Detroiter Max Fisher was about to have his sixtieth birthday. His wife, Marjorie, a beautiful southern belle, decided to give him the surprise party to end all surprise parties—she invited fifty of Max's close friends for a five-day trip to Las Vegas.

Margie had rented a jet, and the guests who had come from London, New York, Chicago and Detroit were already on board when the truly surprised Max walked in and fifty of us shouted, "Surprise!"

The ruse used to get Max Fisher on board that plane was a logical one. Max was told that he was going to meet Michigan's former Governor George Romney for a conference on a plane out at Detroit's Metropolitan Airport. This was not an unusual meeting place for them, so it worked, and that's how Max was literally shanghaied.

Among the fifty guests was the wife of one of the nation's top business tycoons. Her husband had accompanied her from New York to our plane to shout "Surprise" with the rest of us, then he took off on another plane for a meeting in London.

Madame X, as she shall so be named in this story, was accustomed to being the center of attention when accompanied by her important husband. Actually, she does all right on her own, too. She's a very tall and attractive lady. And she owns a very important jewel collection. She has also been nominated to the best-dressed lists. She makes *Women's Wear Daily* and the society columns regularly.

But, everyone on this trip was important to our hosts. Everyone was treated with lavish consideration. I mean, how much better could we have been treated than to be given our own suite, cars at our disposal, valet and laundry bills taken care of, etc., etc.? This time Madame X was not singled out for special attention.

Our hostess had carefully planned for us to see all the shows playing then in Vegas. We were free to come and go as we pleased, except for the fifth and last night when we were all asked to meet (in evening clothes) in the gourmet dining room of Caesar's Palace.

This is when and where Max's actual birthday party was to be celebrated. During dinner, we were told that tables had been reserved for us to see Milton Berle in the main showroom. When I heard this, I took it upon myself to run backstage to tell Milton that we would be sitting ringside at two long tables, and I thought it might be nice if he congratulated Max from the stage.

That was my first mistake!

During dinner we were served four or five different wines. Madame X drank her share. Somehow the wine affected her more than it did the rest of us.

During Milton Berle's show, something (and I attribute it to the wine) impelled the lady to become a part of his act. A part that drove the master of the "put-down," Milton Berle, almost to desperation.

Let me explain in sequence exactly what happened: During the early part of his act, Milton spoke glowingly of Max Fisher's attributes. He told how Mr. Fisher was the president of the U.J.A. in the United

States. He spoke of Max's many charitable contributions and then kidded him about the affluence of all his guests. He also said it was his (Milton's) birthday too.

At that time Berle was trying out a new act with young performers. Alone on a stage he can handle any heckler, but he had never worked with these kids before. Their blackout sketches were not terribly tasteful nor were they particularly funny. Suddenly, during one of the sketches, the tall Madame X stood up at our table in all her splendor, including her diamond chandelier earrings, which were dazzling in the spotlight, and said out loud to Berle, "That's not funny!" Then she sat down.

At still another point in the show, from her seat this time, she mouthed these words to Berle (remember we were sitting almost on the stage): "You stink." He saw what she said. So did the kids in the act.

Milton looked directly down at me, and if looks could kill, I would not be writing this story today.

Leaning across the table I whispered to Madame X, "Keep your mouth shut!"

That was my second mistake! Her loud retort to me was "You and your show-biz friends! I won't keep quiet just because he's a friend of yours. I don't like the act."

From somewhere under the table I felt a kick, which meant "Keep quiet." How could my husband's foot reach me from three seats away?

Our host and hostess sat rigidly in their seats staring at the stage, not daring to look at any of us. Well, if it was attention Madame X wanted, she sure was getting it. Every eye in the room was focused on her instead of on Berle.

Even though Milton was trying out a new act, he used the last twenty minutes he has always used. It's a touching turn where the buffoon turns serious. All alone onstage he takes off his makeup with cold cream and a towel. The orchestra plays in slow tempo

"There's No Business Like Show Business" as he tells the audience why there are no people like show people and how the show must go on, etc.

Also, in this segment, Milton pays tribute to his departed mother, Sandra (Sadie) Berle. No matter how many times you see this part of Berle's act, it is always moving.

Madame X was moved by this part of the show too—moved to speak out these exact words, "Now—it's funny." Oh, brother!!

Milton looked down at me with eyes that spoke a death wish—for *me!!*

When the show was over, I said I had to go backstage to explain the horrifying events of the evening. Our hostess, a true daughter of the South, said she and Max would come along to apologize for the behavior of their one guest.

Hollywood film producer Bob Goldstein, one of Max's best buddies, said, "I wouldn't do that if I were you." Turning to me he asked, "How well do you know Milton?"

"Extremely well," I answered. "My father was the judge who married him to Ruth, his present wife."

Bob Goldstein, obviously, knew Berle a whole lot better than I did. He said, "You haven't seen anything until you've seen Berle's temper. And I have a hunch you are going to see it tonight!"

Paying no attention to such "nonsense," I led the troops backstage. By the "troops," I mean Max and Marjorie Fisher, my husband and Bob Goldstein who came along to pick up the pieces. As I approached the dressing room (the others following behind), Milton's brother, standing outside it, with his arms folded like a bodyguard in a gangster movie, said, "I wouldn't go in there if I were you. I don't think Milton wants to see you."

The others instantly and delightedly turned on their heels to leave. "Nonsense," I insisted. "We must explain things to Milton."

That was mistake number three!

An angry voice shouted, "Is that you, Shirley? Get in here."

I went into the dressing room holding my husband's hand, dragging him along for protection. Then Milton let me have it! He called not only me, but the Max Fishers, who had brought and paid for all fifty of their guests to see him, every four-letter word any of us had ever heard, plus one five-letter word none of us had ever heard. He called the "lady" who had bugged him a "cooze." It took me a year and a half to get the definition of the word "cooze." Somehow from his tone, we figured it meant exactly what I learned it did!

Max waited outside the dressing room, but Marjorie came in and knelt down in front of Berle, who was sitting in a chair looking pathetic, with a towel around his neck and his head in his hands. Marjorie, on her knees, sadly looked up into Berle's hostile eyes and said, "You must forgive that lady. She isn't always like that. Besides, forty-nine of us adored you, Mr. Berryl [southern talk]."

This heaped another chain of four- and five-letter epithets upon us all. Berle, turning then to me, said, "If my wife, Ruth, were at the table, she would have slapped that woman in the face."

This made me mad enough to say (because I was tired of apologizing), "Since I am fortunately not your wife, it was not my prerogative to slap her in the face." Then we all walked out!

Riding back to the hotel in the cab, I figured on two divorces—ours and the Fishers. And Bob Goldstein's "I told you what Milton is like when he's angry" didn't help the situation either.

Max Fisher said, "No one has ever talked to me like that before." Marjorie then turned on Max, saying, "Berryl had every right to be angry." Well, maybe he did, but two wrongs never do make a right.

Edward accused me of starting the whole thing by

going backstage to tell Berle about Max's birthday. By the time we reached the hotel, Max and Margie weren't speaking to each other and neither were Edward and I! I don't think I was even speaking to Goldstein, the innocent bystander! Actually, my husband was right. He felt that it was terrible for our hosts to be subjected to such humiliation by a friend of ours.

This was our last night of what, up until then, had been a fabulous party.

Of course, the next day everyone forgave everyone else—even Madame X was forgiven by everyone—except by me. I didn't talk to her for two years. Normally Madame X is a delightful woman. Maybe the fact that everyone was paired off in couples and she was alone bugged her—especially after several drinks.

I didn't talk to Milton Berle either, until about a year and a half later. I was in Sardi's sitting with Shirley Jones and Jack Cassidy, and Milton stopped by the table and told Shirley and Jack about "that night." He was so funny about it, I had to give in and laugh. Time truly does heal wounds. A year and a half later, the incident turned into a hilarious story. Incidentally, it wasn't until that night at Sardi's, that I learned the definition of the five-letter word "cooze" from Milton Berle himself. He was shocked to discover that neither we nor the Fishers had ever heard the word before. Of course, as soon as he told me, I called Margie in Detroit to tell her. If you don't know the word—get in touch with Berle.

I have since gone backstage to see Milton, although I vowed I never would again. I'll always go to see him perform—but never will I ask for a ringside table if I am with anyone except my husband. He's too adept at lip reading!

# Help—the Doctor Needs Help!

We were having a party at our home in Detroit for Ann-Margret and her husband, Roger Smith. Ann-Margret was opening the following night at the Elmwood Casino in Windsor, Canada (only a tunnel ride from Detroit). Originally, we had planned to invite more than a hundred people. Ann-Margret, who may not seem so, is extremely shy and a little afraid of meeting people, so she asked us please to keep the list down to just a few of our close friends.

Well, when you are entertaining an Ann-Margret, everyone becomes your close friend, so it was difficult to cut the list. We managed, but some seventy people are still not speaking to us.

The party was called for six o'clock. She would have to leave early on account of band rehearsals the next morning.

At five the phone rang. It was Roger Smith, saying, "We just arrived from Los Angeles and I think Ann-Margret has a strep throat. Do you know a doctor we can call?" Since the party was to start in one hour, you can imagine how worried I was.

I remembered that our family doctor and his wife had been invited, so I suggested that Ann-Margret and Roger come on to the party, and we would have a doctor here at the house waiting for them. Roger thought that was a great idea, but he warned me that because his wife was feeling so ill, they probably would have to leave even earlier than planned.

Immediately I called our doctor and asked him to bring along his little black bag and all the antibiotics he had around the house.

That same week, Ann-Margret had been on the covers of *Life* and *Look*. Because of her performance in *Carnal Knowledge* she had suddenly become the hottest current movie name in the business.

Dr. Nathan Schlafer, with black bag in hand, escorted Ann-Margret and Roger upon their arrival up to our bedroom. Naturally, he would have to examine her famous chest. You can imagine the jokes making the rounds downstairs. Those who had already seen *Carnal Knowledge* discussed the measurements of her bosom. Also discussed was the fact that the good and kind doctor would have to give her a shot in her famous derriere. That thought so titillated the boys (I mean men who suddenly became boys) that two of them borrowed white jackets from our rented waiters, went upstairs, knocked on the bedroom door, and said, "Doctor, we heard you call for interns—and here we *are!*"

Later, when Ann-Margret, Dr. Schlafer and Roger came down to join the party, the doctor good-naturedly accepted the jeers, jibes and jokes.

Dr. Schlafer, an older gentleman (and I do mean "gentleman" in the true sense of the word), had to put up with funny and some unfunny cracks at his country club, his city club and from associates at his various hospitals for months after the party. Word had gotten around fast! The only one who didn't tease him was his understanding wife. Ann-Margret did indeed have a temperature that night, and the doctor's red face, as he came down, made him look as though he was the one with fever.

# Oscar Memories

The Oscar nominees for best performance by an actress in a supporting role for 1971 were Ellen Burstyn and Cloris Leachman, each for *The Last Picture Show*, Barbara Harris for *Who Is Harry Kellerman?*, Margaret Leighton for *The Go-Between* and Ann-Margret for *Carnal Knowledge*. Everyone in the industry felt it was a shoo-in for Ann-Margret. The betting, though, about two weeks before the Oscars switched to a tossup between Ann-Margret and Cloris Leachman. The newspapers and magazines all chose Ann-Margret. But Ann-Margret felt the much-coveted award would go to Ellen Burstyn who had already won the New York Critics' Award as best supporting actress.

We had arranged to sit with the Roger Smiths at the Academy Award ball following the telecast. Well—the Academy members voted Cloris Leachman the Oscar. We were already seated at the table in the ballroom of the Beverly Hilton when Roger and Ann-Margret arrived. She had a fixed smile on her face which hid the tears that were waiting to flow. It's not easy having to show up at a victory party when you are a loser. Sitting next to her, I whispered to A-M how sorry I was. Cloris Leachman was marvelous in *The Last Picture Show,* but it is natural to want your friend to win.

Said Ann-Margret, "I knew I wouldn't win! And Cloris deserves her Oscar." She made me feel even sadder when she said that her father, who had been very ill for a long time and was a patient in a nursing home, managed to come to the theatre for the Academy presentations. "I wanted to win for him," she said. "When the award for the best supporting actress was announced, I whispered, 'Daddy, I wish I could have won for you.'"

To be one of the five nominees in any of the Academy categories is a great honor. Yet it's still a terrible let-down, if only for the moment, not to be the winner.

Another poignant moment at this particular Academy Award ball happened when Peter Finch walked head-on into Gene Hackman, with Hackman holding the Oscar he won as best actor, in *The French Connection.* Finch, who had been nominated for his brilliant performance in *Sunday, Bloody Sunday,* embraced Hackman and said, "You deserved to win."

Hackman replied, "I know how you feel. I'm glad I won, but, believe me, I know how you feel!" With that he put his hand gently on Finch's cheek. "Honestly, I know how you feel, Peter, you deserve part of this." And he held the Oscar out to Finch. This was the very first time the two had met.

It was the same evening which brought Charlie Chaplin back to America and to Hollywood after his many years of exile in Europe. At this forty-third Academy Awards presentations, Mr. Chaplin was presented with a special Oscar for his contribution to the motion-picture industry.

With all my heart I believe he deserved this tribute from an industry to which he contributed so much, for so long. But also, with all my heart, I do not believe he deserved to be acclaimed as a homecoming hero to the United States. I did not approve of the standing ovation given to Charlie Chaplin, the man, the night he attended the Metropolitan Opera in New York. This Charlie Chaplin is the same man who continually denounced the United States Government. However, the aging, sick Charlie Chaplin deserved all the huzzas he received on that Monday evening, April 10, 1972.

Our table at the ball was next to the one at which sat the Chaplins, the Gregory Pecks and the Mike Frankoviches. From my vantage point I was able to observe the comings and goings of the many paying homage to Chaplin. And this was right.

Sometime during the evening, Alan King excitedly, with tears in his eyes, said, "He kissed me! Can you believe that Charlie Chaplin said 'I know who you are' and then he kissed my hand." I didn't tell the elated Mr. King that Chaplin had kissed the hands of other visitors to his table. Obviously it was an easier thing for him to do than to speak to each and every person who approached him.

One of the best times I ever had on an Academy Award night (and I have attended every one of them for the past fifteen years) was when we returned to the Polo Lounge of the Beverly Hills Hotel after the Oscar ceremonies and the ball to drink champagne with Mitzi Gaynor and other friends. The musicians who normally play in the Persian Room of the hotel had apparently played elsewhere that night and were returning to the hotel to put their instruments on the bandstand. The Academy Award-winning song that year was "Never on Sunday," which was also the most popular song of the year.

Since the hour was late, the hotel lobby was virtually empty except for our now departing party and the returning musicians.

Mitzi Gaynor began to sing, quietly at first, "Never on Sunday." Then we all joined in. The musicians, getting the feel of the "happening," took up their instruments and started to play along with us. Leaping from chair to chair and now singing at the top of her voice, Mitzi Gaynor led the way, and we all played "follow the leader." So help me, it could have been a scene from any one of Betty Grable's movies. The musicians followed Mitzi and her group all the way out to the cars into which they all piled, still playing and singing "Never on Sunday." Some got into the car with Mitzi and the others into the car behind her. These special times are difficult to describe.

I'm ashamed to admit that I never did check to see whether or not the night manager lost his job because of "Never on Sunday" and all the noise we had made on this Monday night.

# A Visit with Mae West

In 1968, before she made *Myra Breckinridge*, Mae West was one of the most sought-after and hard to get interviews. Youngsters who knew Mae only from the "late" and "late-late shows" were as fascinated by this woman's mystique as I have always been.

Somehow, I managed to find a gentleman who knew her well and persuaded him to get me an interview with the super, superstar in her own home. I don't think I shall ever forget this fascinating woman or my visit in her Hollywood apartment.

When we rang the bell, a great big muscleman answered the door and ushered us into the cream-colored living room.

The muscleman disappeared, but in the living room a young man was superintending the playing of a Mae West recording. "Happy Birthday 21" was the name of the song. As "Happy Birthday 21" played over and over again, I looked around the cream-colored room. There was a Louis XIV couch in her Louis XIV living room, surrounded by dozens of Mae West photos, paintings of Mae West, statues of Mae West and on the piano was (you should pardon the expression) an alabaster bust of Mae West. The room was old world elegance, in spite of three turkish towels with the names of hotels stamped on them, draped over the soft down cushions on the couch.

I learned that the young man's name was Robert Durand, and he was the twenty-one-year-old president of the Mae West Fan Club. This was his avocation; he earned his bread and board by working in the post office.

While listening to Mae sexily singing "Happy Birthday 21" over and over again, I waited with bated breath for something wonderful to happen.

And it did!

Mae herself sashayed into the room with her much-imitated wiggle, wearing a long green and white flowered peignoir. Her first words were addressed to Robert.

"Get up and dance, Rob," she murmured, making it sound like so much more. Robert jumped to his feet.

"Kick high for the lady," she said, which he did to the musical background of "Happy Birthday 21." By now, there wasn't a single note or phrase of that song I hadn't memorized.

"Rob's dancing saves me havin' to get up and do it for you," said Mae.

She then segued over to the turkish towel-covered couch, motioning me to follow, which I did.

I received, and still do, stacks of mail asking me to reveal Miss West's famous beauty secret. I knew what it was, but needed her permission to tell it. She gave me permission, but neither she nor I at the time thought it proper to discuss it in print. However, things have changed since 1968, and I no longer fear using the word—though it's still not that easy for me to write. The elusive word is *enema*. Miss West said she used this type of purgative daily.

Equally as important, she said, to her beauty and health is the fact that she never drinks or smokes, and she refuses to eat fatty foods.

Miss West massages her bosom with cocoa butter,

and she does all her exercising on the bed! If you are thinking what I think you are thinking, you need a purgative for your mind, because Miss West went on to explain that by exercising on the bed, she meant that when she gets up in the morning she tenses her toes, then her ankles, then her legs, then the abdomen and on and on—upwards!

I asked her what kind of men she likes. Mae replied, "I like all sizes, shapes and types. The man I don't like doesn't exist."

If you are a cigar smoker, don't bother to call on Mae. She will not permit a cigar smoking gent near her.

How does Mae West live? Like a queen, I would say. She has the apartment in Hollywood, a ranch that houses her trotters and race horses in the San Fernando Valley, and a Santa Monica twenty-two-room beach house. A chauffeured limousine waits out front to take her wherever she goes. And she has a bevy of young, strong, attractive males attending her every wish and command.

All her domestic help are male. Her male teen-age fans give her diamonds for Christmas and birthdays. Her own jewelry collection, which puts the Gabors' to shame, is worth more than a million dollars. Mae's land is worth more than six times what she paid for it originally.

Part of Mae West's code of honor, and she does have great integrity, has always been: "I never bother with a married man, even though some of our best men are married."

Mae, who was seventy-five years of age when I interviewed her in 1968, had beautiful, white, almost wrinkle-free skin, and her hands were those of a far younger woman.

I asked, "What is the source of all your energy?"

"Would you believe," she answered, "I just recently found out I was born with a double thyroid. I used to wonder why I could stay up all night and wear everyone else out."

Mae is an ESP enthusiast, and has always believed in it.

"Just the other morning, before I actually awoke, a person came to me in my thoughts, and told me not to do something I was gonna do. You know, that person saved me losing one hundred thousand dollars in a law suit?"

"Is there a man in your life now?"

"I always have a few around. Safety in numbers, you know," replied this exciting lady.

I asked her if sex was still important to her.

"What do you think?" she smiled. "Sex is in back of everything you do. Whether a man builds a building or an empire, it's the sex drive behind that does it. Shirley, if your sex and health are gone, men don't want anything from you!"

Then, from nowhere, she took my hand, put it on a strand of her long blond hair, and said, "Pull, pull hard, dearie."

Obviously, she wanted me to know that all that long hair hanging down her back was her very own and not a wig. I pulled hard as she commanded, and she didn't flinch. Then she opened her mouth, showed me the pearly whites, took my hand, and asked me to make a fist, which I did. "Hit 'em," she said. "Hit 'em," knocking my knuckles against her teeth. "Mine," she said pointing to her teeth, "all mine."

Well, they sure didn't fall out when I hit 'em.

At the time I visited Mae she was actually in demand again, for night clubs, movies and television. She was planning to do a television special at Universal, but I don't know what happened to that project. She had also signed to do a movie of *Sextette*, a play she wrote. Don't know what happened to that either. Somehow, I wish she had done her own film, rather than the stupid *Myra Breckinridge* she did do.

She was also being offered engagements at some of

the better hotels on the Las Vegas strip. She told me that the last time she played Vegas, the owner of the hotel not only paid her top money, but he also gave her an eighteen-thousand-dollar diamond and platinum bracelet for doing such big business. She hadn't had that bracelet reappraised in years, but thought it worth much more on today's diamond market.

Before I left Miss West's apartment, which I hated to do because I was having such a marvelous time, she sashayed into her bedroom, motioning to me and the gentleman who had brought me there, to follow. Suddenly, I felt her pushing me onto the emormous canopied bed.

"Oh no," I thought. "This can't be happening. Not Mae West!"

Within seconds, I was lying on top of the bed as Miss West, standing alongside, pointed up and said, "Look up, honey, look up."

There above me was Mae West's own personal Sistine Chapel. All she wanted was for me to see her mirrored ceiling. When I stood up, I asked how I should describe her bedroom with the heavy damask drapes held up by a crown hanging over the pillows.

"Just say," said Mae "that it's all Louis XIV—but Louis never had it so good!"

And neither did I, Miss West. Neither did I!

# Godfather Premiere

Paramount Pictures knew up front what a big winner they had in *The Godfather*. Only a few of us were brought in to New York from out of town for its world première. When a motion picture company opens a movie they aren't sure of, a larger number of press are schlepped in from wherever to be wined and dined at preview or première festivities. I was delighted and flattered to be invited to *The Godfather*.

The postpremière party at the St. Regis was probably one of the gayest ever given. Paramount's producing chieftain Robert Evans hosted the victory bash. Ali McGraw danced so closely with her husband, Bob Evans, I thought she was coming through the other side of him. (Not too long after, Ali left Bob Evans for Steve McQueen.)

All the stars in the film and many others not in the film danced, ate, drank and patted each other on the back. The picture was in the bag, and the bag was filled with money and the money was obviously on its way to the bank!

At the party I sat at a table with Erich Segal, the exhausting young dynamo who only the year before had been the fair-haired boy of the motion-picture industry, especially Paramount Pictures, because of his novel and film *Love Story*. Now only a year later, he seemed to be the forgotten man at this festive *Godfather* victory ball.

As a matter of fact, along with Gordon Parks, Erich and I rode back together from the theatre to the St. Regis. Erich told me in the car that he never again wanted to write a successful commercial venture. He preferred, he said, to again become anonymous and continue to do what he loved best—teach, as he was doing then at Yale. Success had diminished his prestige with his students, and he wished for future students to know him only as their professor.

At the *Godfather* party, it seemed his wish for anonymity was being granted. In the movie world, as in most big-business, the credo is "But, baby, what did you do for me today?"

Andy Williams, who has by now sold more than a million records of the love theme from the *Godfather,* had sold just as many records the year before of the song "Love Story." At the party he was invited to sing the *Godfather* theme, after which the happy crowd shouted for "Love Story." Apparently, the pianist couldn't play it in his key so Andy tried to beg off. When Erich Segal whispered in my ear, "I can play it for him," I called out from the table, "Erich Segal is here and he can play the music for Andy." Bob Evans jumped up on the bandstand, looked over to our table and said, "Come on, Erich. Play it for Andy." Segal suddenly became shy and said he was afraid he couldn't play it well enough, which, of course, was not true. This was the first and only moment to my knowledge that Segal was recognized officially that night by any of the Paramount hierarchy. I don't know if Erich was hurt, but I hurt for him!

Leaving the party, I spotted Nina Van Pallandt and her manager. At the time she was very much in the news. The Clifford Irving story was on the front page

of every paper in the world, and it was the Baroness
Van Pallandt, one of Irving's big loves, who had recently put the finger on him (or should we say, "gave
him the finger?"). It was her testimony which proved
Clifford Irving's biography of Howard Hughes a com-
plete hoax. I chatted with the baroness and her manager, who did most of the talking. Actually, this
beautiful woman was charming and gracious about
answering most of my nitty-gritty questions. Just as
one of the several hundred photographers chanced by
and snapped a picture of the three of us standing
together, actress Jill Ireland (Mrs. Charles Bronson)
walked up, uttered an impolite epithet and threw the
contents of a glass of champagne into Nina's manager's
face, splattering the baroness and this reporter at the
same time. The actress then turned on her heels and
walked away. Nina Van Pallandt may have known
better than I the reason for Mrs. Bronson's outburst,
because she asked no questions. I did! At first he
claimed, "I never met her before in my life." Then
when we all sat down at a table out in the hall, so he
could compose himself, I continued the inquest. After
saying, "I never met her before in my life," his very
next statement was "She hates me from a long time
ago." Then he went on to tell things I cannot print
because I don't know if they are true.

That entire episode was jarring to the nerves, especially for Nina's manager. But I wouldn't have
missed it for the world!

Some six months later, while waiting for our cars in
front of the Beverly Hills Hotel, once again I saw
Baroness Nina Van Pallandt. She wore dark glasses
and looked very much like the movie star she might
become, and she was accompanied by a secretary.
I reintroduced myself as we stood there talking.
"Baroness, how do you feel, knowing that your testimony had so much to do with both Mr. and Mrs.
Irving being sentenced to jail [their sentence had
been handed down by the court just the day before]?"

"I'd rather not say," she replied with a lovely grin that stretched from ear to ear. "My testimony is just something that had to be done." I could get no further on that subject.

Nina was willing, however, to discuss the movie she was making with Elliott Gould, called *The Long Goodbye*. She said she adored being in movies and hoped to do more. Well, I'd hoped to do more third-degreeing, but her car drew up and away she went, secretary, dark glasses and all, leaving me behind, thinking about her ear-to-ear grin.

# Western Union Is a Fink

I had a chance to make some extra loot simply by lunching with Shirley Jones in the Polo Lounge of the Beverly Hills Hotel.

As we dined on McCarthy salads (the Beverly Hills Hotel's secret recipe), Shirley told me that she and Jack Cassidy were separating—this time for good. Since I adore Shirley and love Jack (although sometimes I could spank him for not realizing how lucky he is to be married to her), Shirley's statement saddened me.

"I won't print anything in the column if there is the slightest chance that you and Jack will get together; but if not, it's my duty in spite of our close friendship, to tell it."

Shirley Jones said, "The news is bound to leak out, and I'd rather you had it than someone else. What's more, I don't plan to sit home and wait for him to come back this time. I want to date."

She should have been charged advertising rates simply for using my column to announce to eligible gentlemen that she was separated and datable.

As we sat at the table talking, Buddy, the hotel's

famous page boy, came over and said, "Call for you, Miss Eder."

On the other end of the phone, a voice whispered, "I'm with such-and-such fan magazine. Whatever Shirley Jones is telling you, we'll buy your story."

I repeated out loud the conversation as it was taking place.

"Why are you whispering?" I asked.

The voice replied, "I don't want Miss Jones to hear me."

"Where are you?" I inquired as I looked around the room.

"I'm back in my office on Sunset Boulevard, but I saw you while I was lunching in the Polo Lounge."

I explained that I was not interested in selling the story to anyone. Shirley Jones, having heard my end of the conversation, laughed.

Five minutes later, back came Buddy saying there was another call for me. This, of course, meant two tips for him. Shirley could have at least kicked in with half, since both calls had to do with her.

The strange voice on the other end said, "I represent such-and-such fan magazine. Are Shirley Jones and Jack Cassidy separating?"

"Where are you?" I asked.

"I'm in my office in New York," said the telephone voice, "and we just got a tip that Shirley looked as though she was confiding in you at the Polo Lounge."

So that my luncheon companion could hear everything, I loudly asked, "How much do you pay for such a story?"

He replied, "Oh, we can go up to fifteen hundred dollars. We pay high."

"Oh," I exclaimed indignantly, "I wouldn't sell a friend down the river for less than ten thousand dollars."

"Well," said the voice on the other end, " we couldn't pay anybody that—even if you told us it was Jackie and Ari who were getting the divorce." He hung up abruptly.

Shirley invited me to dinner at her house that night, saying there would only be a few friends.

Later, when I rang her doorbell, I couldn't have been more shocked. The door was opened by Jack Cassidy, who gave me a big kiss, then brought me into the living room, acting very much the host, and still the master of the house.

At dinner, he sat in his chair at the head of the table. Ruth Aarons, Shirley and Jack's manager, called to say there was an Associated Press story out confirming their separation. Jack indignantly turned to Shirley saying, "How did that leak? No one was to know."

"I don't know," exclaimed Shirley. "I just told Shirley Eder at lunch, and she's not with Associated Press."

It puzzled me too, because I had wired the scoop into the Detroit *Free Press* as late as five o'clock that afternoon for the next morning's edition. The paper couldn't possibly have reached the streets.

That's it! The wire! I had gone to the Beverly Hills Western Union Telegraph Office, as I normally do, to send the column. Obviously, there was a "stoolie" in that particular Western Union office! Actually, a man I had never seen there before or since accepted the wire.

Jack was angry that Shirley had told even me, though he was the one who wanted out of the marriage. He felt he wasn't able to concentrate properly on his own career. He didn't want his leaving again publicized, I'm sure, so that he could come back home (as was his habit) without having to save face.

"Why," he said angrily, "did you even tell Shirley Eder?"

"It's very simple," replied Shirley Jones. "This time, Jack, I want it known that I'm going to date! I'm just not going to sit around waiting for you to come home!"

A few days later in Detroit, I told my husband what Shirley had said about dating.

"Hey," he exclaimed, "give me her number. I want to be first in line."

That much of a friend to Shirley Jones I'm not!

As of this writing, the Cassidys have reconciled again. By the time this book is published, they will have separated and reconciled many times over. They happen to be very much in love with each other, but it's a tough go for a husband and wife to be involved in the ego-building and deflating business called show business.

# Hollywood Party Time

I've been to a lot of parties all over the world, but never to one more glamorous than the dinner dance given prior to the Motion Picture Relief Fund gala by twelve hostesses in the Beverly Hills home belonging to Polly Bergen and Freddie Fields. The hostesses included Mrs. Jack Benny, Mrs. Freddie Brisson (Rosalind Russell), Mrs. Armand Deutsch, Mrs. David May, Mrs. Walter Mirisch, Mrs. Jerry Orbach, Mrs. Gregory Peck, Mrs. Jules Stein, and Bonita Granville Wrather.

The party was given for the out-of-town guests of the hostesses who had come to California from all over the world for the gala. In spite of the worthy cause (all monies went to the Motion Picture Relief Fund), the actual reason people flew in from everywhere was to attend the final "onstage" performance of Frank Sinatra, who was to bid us farewell as a performer at the gala the following night.

The one line I loved on the invitation read "Dress Casually Beautiful."

This meant "Don't come to the party looking like a slob!"

As I looked around the heated tent-enclosed patio,

the array of stars eating, drinking and dancing should happen at the yearly Oscar awards, where so many of the really big names ought to, but never do, show up.

For openers, there was Princess Grace of Monaco, who was not wearing a tiara, but looked so regal, my mind's eye supplied one on her head. (A little side note on the eating habits of the princess—she eats tacos with her fingers even as you and I.)

Andy Williams arrived at the party with his buddy and house guest Ted Kennedy. Andy introduced me to Ted that night. Publicist Warren Cowan came with Raquel Welch, but lost her somewhere during the evening to the former MGM boss, handsome Bo Polk. Polk kept scurrying back and forth bringing Raquel goodies from the buffet table. I still don't know which swain got to take her home. Actually, all the gals had to shift for themselves on line at the buffet tables. All —that is, except Raquel Welch and her Serene Highness, the Princess Grace of Monaco. Ryan O'Neal came to the bash single-o. At the time, I had heard that O'Neal and Andy Williams' estranged wife, Claudine Longet, were seeing each other—off screen. Ali Mc-Graw held hands all night long with her then husband, Robert Evans. Remember, this party was in 1971. Ruth Berle came without Milton, who was in the East cohosting the "Mike Douglas Show."

Jennifer Jones introduced her brand-new (at the time) husband, millionaire Norton Simon. Polly Bergen never stopped dancing to the music of the two bands: Lionel Hampton's and the all-girl group Fanny.

Don Rickles must have been "on" for the help manning the buffets because they kept laughing as he moved down the line. Gregory and Veronique Peck told me that over eight hundred thousand dollars' worth of tickets had been sold, and that the total money raised for that first Motion Picture Relief Fund benefit exceeded one million dollars. The Motion Picture Fund, I hope, bowed low, thanked and blessed

Frank Sinatra for choosing to retire officially the night of their big bash.

I sat at a table with Shirlee and Henry Fonda, Gloria and Jimmy Stewart, and Lucille Ball and her husband, Gary Morton. Lucy was reminiscing about the times she and Ginger Rogers double-dated bachelors Henry Fonda and Jimmy Stewart.

Neither Henry nor Jimmy nor Lucy could remember which girl went out with what fella, but Lucy laughingly recalled that although the boys did take them dancing at the posher places in Los Angeles, like the Cocoanut Grove and the Mocambo, they didn't invite them to eat there. Instead they always took Ginger and Lucy after dancing to a joint called Barney's Beanery.

Lucy, Hank and Jimmy laughed out loud while remembering. Lucy slapped her thigh and blurted out, "Hey, do you remember that after you fed Ginger and me at Barney's, Hank, you and Jimmy would then take us back home to your shared pad, where you'd lower the lights in the living room and then usher us into the kitchen to wash the dishes, which had been stacked up in the sink for a week!"

Tears ran down the boys' eyes from laughing, as they remembered. They may have been young, but they were already big stars at the time.

When I told Ginger, who was not at the Fields' house that night, the story Lucy had told us, she laughed as hard as the others did.

"Yes," said Ginger, "Lucy told the truth. We actually did wash all their stacked-up dirty dishes."

W-e-l-l, Fonda and Stewart may have been big stars, but they were also big "cheapies!" I suppose if you looked like Stewart or Fonda did, you wouldn't have to spend much money on a gal either. But let's face it, Ginger Rogers and Lucille Ball weren't exactly what the fellas used to call "dog dates."

Hank Fonda told us about the first big party he attended when he came out to California from the New York stage.

"I looked all around the room at the big stars and wished I could go to a phone to call home to my family in Nebraska and say, 'Hey, do you know who I'm with?'"

Well, that night at Freddie and Polly Fields's house, I felt like calling home and saying, "Hey, look at me. See who I'm with."

It was a good thing there were twelve hostesses to kick in with the loot to help defray the expenses, because other than the Charlotte and Anne Ford (daughters of Henry Ford II) coming-out parties, this was probably the most extravagant bash I had attended.

About Sinatra's farewell performance, my goose bumps are still showing. He sang with his heart, his head and his guts. He made musical sounds he hadn't made since he was a skinny kid singing to thousands of screaming teen-agers all over America.

The many name stars who performed at the gala, had no choice in picking the spot on the program where they would appear. But I'm told Barbra Streisand demanded she be on next to closing, just before Sinatra. Believe me, that's where she belonged. Only Sinatra, this night, could have equaled Barbra. She, too, had never been in better voice.

There were Durante, and Jack Benny, and Jimmy Stewart, and Pearl Bailey, and Rock Hudson, and David Niven, and Sammy Davis, and Jack Lemmon, and Don Rickles, and Greg Peck, and Grace Kelly, and Cary Grant and on and on. It was a once-in-a-lifetime kind of program.

Frank had eight cameras spotted around the theatre filming his farewell appearance. Prints were to be given to each of his children, and several saved for his future grandchildren. See what I mean about my goose bumps showing?

P.S. Only recently, Mr. Sinatra decided to come out of retirement. His friends say it was because he was bored.

# The Cab Driver and the Lady

This may be difficult to believe, but Helen Hayes, the "first lady" of the American Theatre, who, like Caesar's wife, has always been above reproach, had a strange man stay in her home overnight!

Shocking as it may seem—it's so! And this is the story:

One day in Chicago, at the Ambassador Hotel, where Miss Hayes was to receive the Sarah Siddons Award (Chicago's top theatrical honor), we lunched together at the famous Pump Room. Miss Hayes exclaimed: "Oh, you are from Detroit. I wonder if you know a man named Henry Adler? He's from Detroit, too. Henry's a good friend of mine. As a matter of fact, he just left me here at the airport to go back to Detroit."

I didn't know her Henry Adler, but I sniffed a romance. To a columnist this kind of conversation spells "romance."

Miss Hayes continued, "Henry drives a taxi for the Detroit Cab company. And he just spent the night with me at my home in upper Nyack, New York. Are you sure you haven't met him?"

W-e-l-l. That was quite an admission from a lady in

her seventies. Mentally, I was delighted for her and gave her credit for having a "gentleman caller" at this time in her life and what's more, being proud of it. Miss Hayes continued, "Why don't you look him up when you get home?"

You can be sure that as soon as I got back to Detroit that's exactly what I did!

Tracking Henry down wasn't easy. I discovered he was between homes, because the one he owned at the address Miss Hayes gave me was being demolished, making way for a new high school. We managed to find him through a message in one of our columns. Subsequently, he showed up, asking for me at the Detroit *Free Press*.

I told him I wanted to know all about his association with the great Helen Hayes. He said he would never exploit his friendship with "Mrs. MacArthur." It took a great deal of convincing on my part to make him believe that it was Miss Hayes herself who asked me to look him up.

It seems the friendship between the actress and the cab driver began in 1961 at the stage door of the Fisher Theatre after a performance of a Shakespeare gig in which Miss Hayes was performing with Maurice Evans. That night Henry Adler and his cab drove her back to her hotel.

After that, Henry made himself available to drive the star and her secretary Miss Vera (as Henry called her) to and from the theatre each night. Henry, who had never seen her on stage, was so taken with Miss Hayes that he refused to accept money for the cab rides. Oh, he had to put his meter on, but he himself paid the cab company the price of the ride out of his own pocket. No matter how his two lady passengers argued with him, there was no way they could get him to accept their money.

So how did Henry progress from simply driving Miss Hayes to her hotel in Detroit to the point of his staying overnight at her Hudson River digs?

Henry explained the succession of events: it seems he picked up the phone in Detroit and called Miss Hayes at her home in Nyack to say he was coming into New York just to see her in the play *The Front Page*, which was then being revived on Broadway. Could she possibly get him a ticket for that night's performance? He also informed her that he would fly back to Detroit right after the show.

"Henry," exclaimed Miss Hayes, "of course you can have a ticket. But, you will *not* fly back to Detroit the same night. I want you to see my home. You are to spend the night in Nyack."

Sooo, Henry bought himself a first-class ticket to New York. He told me, "I always travel first class. You see, I just charge it. I have a charge account with the airlines."

Henry Adler arrived at the Ethel Barrymore Theatre only to learn that there had been no ticket left in his name. "There must be some mistake," he told the suspicious theatre treasurer. Indeed there had been. After calling backstage to Miss Hayes, the treasurer discovered that the ticket had accidentally been placed under "H" for Henry, instead of "A" for Adler.

Not too many of us have the courage to go backstage to visit a star in his or her dressing room before curtain time. But Henry visited with the first lady of the American theatre in her dressing room before the show, by invitation.

After the show, he, Miss Hayes, Miss Vera and two poodles piled into a station wagon which was parked outside the stage door. With Vera at the wheel, off they went across the George Washington Bridge to Nyack. "Miss Vera," said our cabby, "drives well enough to be a cab driver herself."

According to Henry, when they arrived at the house, they all sat in the kitchen drinking coffee. Miss Hayes, or Mrs. MacArthur, as Henry respectfully speaks of her, said, "Good night," then went up to her bedroom, after which Miss Vera escorted Henry into the guest suite.

When he awakened at seven the next morning, no one else was up, so he wandered around the property. Then around ten, Miss Hayes appeared and asked Henry, who weighed more than three hundred pounds at the time, what he would like for breakfast. "Anything you got handy, Mrs. MacArthur. I'm not fussy."

So "herself" made him bacon and eggs and toast and coffee. Miss Hayes lives in the house with her secretary and a housekeeper who does not cook. Tiny, dynamic Helen Hayes cooks for herself and her staff.

Henry laughed as he recalled his hostess saying, "Now I'll autograph your eggs for you," as she lay three slices of bacon over the eggs forming the letter "H."

"You know," he said, "I just sat there and said, 'Mrs. MacArthur, no one will ever believe this. Just no one!'"

After breakfast, Helen Hayes said she had to fly to Chicago where she was to receive the Sarah Siddons Award (her second). Henry asked, "Do you mind if I keep you company as far as Chicago? Then, I'll change planes and go on home to Detroit."

She didn't mind, so Henry Adler flew side-by-side with the great star to Chicago. Because he weighs so much, the stewardess had to replace his seat belt with an extra long one they always carry on board for extra fat passengers. Miss Hayes is so tiny, he actually could have borrowed part of hers.

Henry said good-by to his friend at the O'Hare Airport where she was met by a committee of "Sarah Siddons" ladies. "Didja kiss her good-by?" we probed.

"No! I wanted to, but didn't think it would look nice at the airport."

"Do you call her Helen?" I asked.

"No, not Mrs. MacArthur," said the shocked Henry. "She commands respect. Mrs. MacArthur is a *great* lady."

"How come you're still a bachelor?"

"Oh, I was married once," he replied, "but now I'm a happy single man."

Henry Adler told me he had placed himself on the election slate several years before, and ran for city councilman. He spent eight hundred dollars for his campaign and received more than three thousand votes.

He would not accept Social Security because he likes working for his money.

Aside from Miss Hayes, Henry has driven lots of celebrity visitors in Detroit. His other favorite is Kay Medford. He used to baby-sit for her dog while she was performing in *Bye, Bye Birdie* at the Fisher. When Albert Deckker was starring there in *A Man for All Seasons*, Henry drove him home each night, first stopping across the street at Topinka's, where they would each have one beer.

What were Henry Adler's immediate plans? "First I'm going to Weight Watchers, because Mrs. MacArthur said to me, 'Henry, you have put on too much weight.' Then, I hope to be in shape to visit Mrs. MacArthur up in Ann Arbor when she gets there in January to rehearse in *Harvey* with Jimmy Stewart. She invited me to come up and see her in the show."

I hate to end this tale of the cab driver and the lady with a cliffhanger, but honestly we never followed the story further. I must remember to ask Miss Hayes, next time we meet, if she ever hears from Henry Adler—And did he lose the weight he had promised her he would?

# Love Letter to a City

From May 4 to June 5, 1971, Henry Fonda came to the Fisher Theatre in Detroit to try out a new play called *The Trial of A. Lincoln.* He deservedly got great personal reviews, yet the critics and the audiences didn't care very much for the play. Ticket buyers came primarily to see Hank Fonda.

During the tryout, Henry had to make up his mind whether or not he would go on to Broadway with it. He felt the play couldn't make it in New York, but the producers said they wouldn't take *A. Lincoln* in without him as its star.

Fonda is the kind of person who cares deeply about theatre and cares equally as much for his fellow performers. The whole time he was in Detroit he carried the burden of "Do I or do I not go to Broadway with the play?" It was his decision to make.

Other stars in the same position would have told producers immediately, "The hell with it! I'm not going in." Hank Fonda worried about putting his actors out of work. He worried too about the producer's investment. Fonda is a concerned man.

Working in *A. Lincoln* every night and rehearsing new lines and scenes during the day, plus the worry

of "Do I or don't I," might have soured him on the city.
It didn't. Hank Fonda loved Detroit. In fact, he so appreciated the kindnesses he received during those five
weeks in Motor City that a few days before he left,
he said, "Shirley, I want to send a 'thank-you' letter
to the city of Detroit. If I sent the letter to you, would
you print it in your column?"

Would I? Of course I would! This is the first time
in my experience as a journalist that an actor has ever
written a "thank-you" note to a city.

Here is the letter which was written in Henry's own
hand:

"Dear Shirley,

"Over the years I have played most of the principal
cities in the country on national tours and I have always enjoyed the experience. But until our recent
visit to Detroit and the Fisher Theatre, it has never
occurred to me to thank a city for its hospitality. We
came here with quite a controversial play we knew
would not please everybody. But the response has
been beyond our wildest dreams.

"However, it is not just the very warm reception we
have been enjoying at the theatre which has prompted
me to write this (and I know I can speak for the whole
company), it's the warm hospitality and generosity we
have felt in the city itself. Everyone has gone out of
his way to make our stay enjoyable. I can't possibly
list everyone who entertained us in his home, etc., but
certainly the Leland House (where the Fondas
stayed) has made it a happy home for most of the
company.

"Lefty and Henry of the Normandie Restaurant
were hosts to the whole cast for supper every Tuesday,
Thursday and Saturday.

"Ken Nicholson of Topinka's went out of his way
for all of us in his wonderful Sardi's-like restaurant.
And the Carrot Patch (health food shop) literally
flooded us with healthy goodies to make us feel welcome. I guess that's the operative word—everyone

made it a point that we should feel *welcome*. We got the message.

"Thank you, thank you, thank you.

"Shirlee and Henry Fonda"

Hank Fonda will always do well as an actor in Detroit. However, even if he doesn't want to do another play in Motor City, after that letter he can always come back and run for Governor of Michigan.

# I Like Barbra Streisand!

Columnists and newspaper people have difficulty interviewing Barbra Streisand. For openers, it's tough to get to Barbra. It was especially so when she first arrived in Hollywood to re-create on film her fantastic Broadway portrayal of Fanny Brice in *Funny Girl*. Fortunately, I never had trouble getting to this star—and I do mean STAR!

Her accessibility to this reporter cannot be attributed to my personal charm or clout. When I first moved to Detroit from New York, Sam and Lester Gruber, who own the Caucus Club and the London Chop House, two restaurants known world wide, kept calling me to come to the Caucus Club to hear a new young singer whom they thought definitely was going places. Her name was Barbra Streisand.

I never did make it in to see her during the many weeks she played there. Later, I did see her as the very funny Miss Marmelstein in the Broadway show *I Can Get It For You Wholesale*. In it she was a great singing comedienne, but I never expected her to become a leading lady. A "superstar" leading lady, at that.

Then came *Funny Girl*. After it, one didn't have to

be clairvoyant to know a new "real" star was here to stay.

Time went by and Miss Streisand, after finishing her Broadway stint in the show, took *Funny Girl* to London. After some time, she went on to Hollywood to make the film.

Her press agent, my good friend Lee Solters from New York, made arrangements with the unit publicist of *Funny Girl* (Carol Shapiro) for me to interview Barbra Streisand on the set, even though it was a closed set with Miss Streisand adamant about not seeing press.

For no other reason except perhaps that she had become so successful, columnists, especially Joyce Haber of the Los Angeles *Times*, pinged away at her in print. They wrote that she was fighting with the director. That she wanted everything her own way. That she insisted on doing her own makeup. And that she didn't like anybody, and certainly nobody liked her.

I walked onto the set of *Funny Girl* at the Columbia Pictures lot, chaperoned by Miss Shapiro, who whispered, "She knows you're coming, but let's stand off here in the corner until I feel the time is right to approach her." Definitely, everyone seemed in awe of "Funny Girl."

About thirty minutes later, Carol whispered, "I'll go tell her you're here. I hope she'll see you!" But Carol never got the chance; at that very moment, Barbra Streisand, having seen me out of the corner of her eye, walked over to where we were standing, put out her hand and said, "Hi, Shirley Eder. I can't thank you enough for those hot dogs."

And that was the secret of my success with Barbra Streisand. The magic words were "hot dogs!"

Barbra Streisand was an aficionado of Nathan's hot dogs. Not too many people know that all Nathan's hot dogs were really made at the time by Hygrade Food Products Corp., and at that time my husband was executive vice-president of the company (he later became president). Most newspapers carried the story of Barbra Streisand's cast party for her London company of *Funny Girl,* saying that she had flown in Nathan's hot dogs from the States.

And this is how it happened: One day I received a long-distance call from Lee Solters, saying, "Shirley, I need help. Your husband, Edward, is the only one I know who can help me. Barbra's closing-night party in London, two nights from now, will be a fiasco unless you come to her rescue. She ordered several hundred pounds of hot dogs to be shipped from New York via air to London. Nathan's okayed the order, and now because of some red tape they can't come through. Barbra is terribly upset."

It seems that some government regulation stipulates that only the processor or the packer is permitted to ship a large meat order out of the country, and Nathan's were not the processors, they were only the middlemen.

I immediately called my husband at his office to ask him for help. When his secretary said he was involved in an important meeting and couldn't come to the phone, I asked her to tell him, "This is an emergency!"

Two minutes later he called back in a panic. "Are you all right? What happened?" When I told him what the emergency was, he got so mad I figured there was no way for Miss Streisand to get those hot dogs in time for the party.

An hour later, a much calmer husband called back and said, "Okay, give me the details on the Streisand order." And at the time he wasn't even a Streisand fan. But I was. I got Lee Solters to call him with the details. Forty-eight hours later Barbra was feeding her guests the several hundred pounds of Nathan's hot dogs.

It turned out to be the party of the year from what I read via the UPI and AP. Even the television newsmen gave space to Barbra and her hot dog party, and

Nathan's got enough coverage from these stories to make them internationally famous. Since Nathan's was a good customer, Edward was delighted not to have his name or Hygrade's attached to the news.

Solters told Barbra the whole story of how she got the weenies, and apparently she had been grateful. From that day to this, it has never been difficult—at least *too* difficult—for me to see her.

We talked for a long time at our first meeting, much to the amazement of the *Funny Girl* cast and crew. At the time I found her shy, yet honest. Barbra told me the reason she refused to see most press was because everything she said was misquoted, and everything she did seemed to be misunderstood, at least in the papers.

Over the years, most of this antagonism against Barbra Streisand seems to have dissipated itself. In turn, she has become much more co-operative with reporters, though she still isn't overjoyed having to meet with them.

That first day we met, I stayed to watch her work. She worked hard! True, she stopped several times to ask veteran director William Wyler for explanations of his many directions, but he seemed happy enough to explain things to her. Later he told me that he found Barbra most co-operative throughout the making of *Funny Girl.* Sure, she had her own ideas on how to play the part, but he had no objections to that. After all, she played the same role on the stage for several years. Many times he compromised; many times she had to compromise.

I remember asking her at that first meeting if it was true that she insisted on doing her own makeup. She said yes that it was. She felt she knew what was right for her peculiar type of face. Whether or not she took some advice in this department, I don't know, but she sure came out looking great in the movie!

During that first interview with Barbra, I was wearing one of those inexpensive enormous-faced watches, which I had bought at Lederer's on Fifth Avenue in New York. She flipped over the watch. So I called the store and had one sent to her. It was so inexpensive I could afford to be a sport. She sent such a beautiful "thank you" note you'd think I'd sent her a watch from Harry Winston's. What's more, she wore our watch for a long time.

Barbra Streisand was making *Hello, Dolly!*, when I visited the Twentieth Century-Fox lot to see actors in another film. While lunching in the commissary, I spotted the *Dolly* unit publicist and went over to ask him if I could see Barbra just to say hello.

He looked at me as I were some kind of nut! "That's absolutely impossible," he said. "She isn't seeing anyone. What's more, an appointment with her cannot be made through the studio. It first has to be requested through her own publicity people."

"Would you do me a favor?" I asked. "Please just tell her I'm here and merely want to say 'Hi'." This poor unit publicist like "lucky Pierre" was really stuck in the middle. He didn't want to cross me and he was scared to death to approach Barbra about me.

He must have figured, "What the hell," one way or the other he was up the creek, because he got up and went to the telephone. Minutes later, with the look of an unbeliever, he said, "Miss Streisand wants to know can you come right over to her dressing room and if so, I'm to bring you there."

Barbra was sitting in the dining room of her bungalow having lunch with her baby son, Jason. Jason's face may have been covered with spinach, but he was so appealing you couldn't help but hug him as he immediately put his spinached face up for a kiss. If an artist could have captured the ecstatic expression on Barbra's face as she looked at her son (it was so filled with love) he'd probably be likened to Renoir or some other painter of that stature.

Barbra, the proud mother, had Jason do "his turn"

for the visitor. She got him to sing. He really was able to sing several of the songs from *Hello, Dolly!*. This delightful scene of mother and child (at times she sang along with him) showed me a side of Streisand few in my business are privileged to see.

The unit publicist waited outside the bungalow. I only stayed a short time because I knew Barbra had to get back to work. As he walked me back to the car he said, "Do you know you are the first person she has seen since we started making *Hello, Dolly!*."

Barbra should write the definitive book on "How to Be a Jewish Mother." When she went to Africa on location for *Up the Sandbox*, Jason, now six years old, went with her. She promised he could dig for relics when they got there. Young Jason was so excited about excavating that he traveled with shovels and all the proper paraphernalia of a junior archaeologist.

Just so Jason wouldn't be disappointed in the event he dug up nothing, Barbra carried in her luggage, a bag of chicken bones to bury in the places where Jason was to dig.

No one can ever knock Barbra Streisand to me. Although I do not find her brimming over with warmth, I have always found her polite, honest and, even today, somewhat shy.

# Parties I Remember

Movie producer Joe Pasternak, who reigned in the halcyon days of MGM, and his wife, Dorothy, invited us to an "intimate" informal dinner party where Joe, a true Hungarian, cooked his famous Hungarian goulash. The guest list was small in size, but not in stature.

For instance, José Iturbi and his sister Amparo were there, as were Judy Garland and Sid Luft, Cornell Wilde and his wife, Jean Wallace, Mr. and Mrs. Tony Randall, Kathryn Grayson, and Jayne Mansfield with her beau Mickey Hargitay.

I remember the cocktail hour running interminably long because Jayne and Mickey were interminably late. Our hosts had just said that we would start dinner without them when the doorbell rang, and Jayne and Mickey made their entrance—and I mean EN-TRANCE!

A former Mr. America, Mickey Hargitay came into the living room with one hand raised above his head and balanced by her tummy on top of that hand was Jayne Mansfield. The only thing missing from this circuslike entrance was the barker and a roll on the drums.

During dinner we all sat around the dining room table talking. After dessert, right there in the dining room, Mickey and Jayne began a gymnastic exhibition. I mean she did a handstand on his shoulders. And he did some lifts and turns, narrowly missing the tables and chairs and thus saving his skull.

Not one of us moved during their performance—we were all much too fascinated by the gall of the performers.

At last Judy Garland who, during cocktail hour, had been sipping water glasses filled with Jack Daniels, exclaimed, "My God, this place is beginning to smell like Terry Hunt's Gym." And it truly had begun to smell like a gymnasium after basketball practice.

We all wandered back into the living room. Somehow Mickey's Mr. America physique was a challenge to the other male guests. Cornell Wilde did push-ups. Sid Luft tried lifting a chair with one hand by the base of its leg. Tony Randall did something, I don't know what, that made him grunt and groan. My husband tried lifting me, but he couldn't because I had eaten too much goulash.

Judy Garland, then in one of her "fat" periods, laughingly bet Hargitay that he couldn't balance her even with his two hands.

Nastily, but still smiling, Jayne retorted, "You're right! He was able to lift Mae West, but I doubt if he could lift you." That did it! That started the glorious hostility which continued between Garland and Mansfield throughout the rest of the evening.

"Oh yes," said Judy. "I had forgotten that Mickey's claim to fame is that he was one of Mae West's musclemen. I remember reading that she was suing you for stealing her Mr. America away from her. That took a lot of doing, didn't it? I mean having to steal a guy away from a much older woman."

Host Pasternak, feeling tempers rising, jumped in and asked José Iturbi if he would honor us all by playing the piano. I guess he thought music could soothe and smooth away all the ill feelings.

Mr. Iturbi played just for us, and it was thrilling. But as soon as he finished one piece, Jayne Mansfield sat down next to him on the piano bench and began to pick out a tune.

"Would you like to play something?" politely asked the world-famous pianist.

"Yes, I would," replied the brazen Jayne.

Iturbi moved away from the piano, leaving center stage to Miss Mansfield, who immediately played a composition she obviously learned as a child. Now that took guts. We were all too awed by the cheekiness of it to even comment, at least until after she went home!

Then someone asked Kathryn Grayson to sing. Mr. Iturbi said, "I will play for you, Kathryn." She sang movingly "The Song Is You" and then "You Are Love" from *Show Boat*.

Would you believe, when they finished, Jayne Mansfield had the nerve to go back to the piano and attempt to play another piece?

Judy, sipping a water glass filled with Jack Daniels (and who could blame her?), kept making funny asides during Jayne's infantile-like performance. Someone suggested that Judy sing. She refused, saying, "I will but [alluding to Jayne] not until that 'nafka' leaves."

At this point, Jayne, having finished her act, said that she and Mickey had to go on to someplace else, and off they went.

After lots of funny cracks from everyone about the departed guests, José returned to the piano to play for Judy who sang up a storm. She was in great voice.

It was a party to remember for two reasons. One— the hijinks of a personality named Jayne Mansfield. And the other—of my being able to sit in someone's living room listening to Judy Garland sing her heart out just for the lucky few of us there.

# A Dim-bright Spotlight

Needless to say, after the Pasternak party, we all thought Jayne Mansfield and her antics ridiculous. Through the years we continued to read about Jayne. Somehow, though, through these same years, I became fond of her.

After she and Mickey Hargitay got married and had children, I went to their home to interview them. Jayne took me through her Sunset Boulevard estate.

In the living room there was a fountain which spouted champagne. (Did you expect water?) The enormous handmade dining-room table, Jayne told me proudly, Mickey had built with his own hands. At the bottom of the Olympic-size swimming pool there was a tiled heart with the words, if I remember correctly, "I love you, Jayne," in the center of it. It had been engraved there in Mickey's handwriting. Their bed was big enough to sleep a dozen people. It, too, was heart shaped, so was their baby son's crib.

That day they offered me soft drinks because Jayne said she and Mickey did not approve of hard liquor and refused to serve it in their home. It was said sincerely, and I was impressed.

221

Jayne-Marie, her little daughter from a past marriage, was polite and well brought up.

Oh, I forgot to mention that in the master bedroom there was a *prie-dieu* on which the family knelt together for nightly prayers.

Obviously, I had come in upon a religious period in Jayne Mansfield's ever-changing life. She was warm and outgoing, and you couldn't help but like her.

I also got to know that Jayne Mansfield was extremely bright, in spite of all the seemingly stupid things she did. These unorthodox actions were designed to bring attention to herself, which they certainly did. What's more, they also gave her the career in show business she so obviously wanted.

Another memorable meeting with Jayne and Mickey took place at the Americana Hotel in Miami Beach. My husband was there for a supermarket convention. Somewhere in Miami I had bumped into Jayne and invited her to dinner with us at the hotel, after which we planned to go on to the jai alai matches. As was her custom, Jayne and her husband arrived over an hour late. This meant we would arrive at the Jai Alai Fronton, if we got there at all, for only the last few games.

When we got up to leave the table after dinner in the Gaucho Room, Jayne in a stage whisper said "Oh my, I think my dress has split right in the middle of my fanny." She was wearing a very low-cut velvet dress, exposing much of her famous bosom. What a spectacle she would make with little on in front, and nothing at all on the backside.

I circled to see just how extensive the damage was and quickly saw that Jayne was wearing absolutely nothing except the velvet dress and shoes!

"What can we do?" she squealed.

My conservative husband, who wasn't too thrilled about any part of the evening, said, "Well, we certainly can't go on to the games. I suggest you and

Mickey go home so you can change your outfit and we'll see you some other time."

It was now after 10 P.M. "No," replied Jayne. "As we came in, I saw a shop here in the hotel next to the restaurant. I'll just go in there and buy something new to wear. You see," she continued, "we have to go to the Fronton because I promised to present a cup to the best player of the evening."

This called for strategy meeting. How could we get up and walk out of the Gaucho Room, much less into the shop, without exposing Jayne Mansfield's tushie to the many who were already staring.

Mickey, well over six feet tall, said he would stand behind his wife with his hands on her shoulders and they would walk out together in tandem. Edward walked far enough away to look as though he had never seen any one of us before in his life.

Fortunately, the shops in the posh Miami Beach hotels stay open late into the night. So Jane walked into a fitting room with three or four salesladies in attendance. When she came out to look at herself in a full-length mirror, she must have noticed through the reflection in the glass that several dozen people had gathered to see her, but she pretended not to see them.

While waiting outside the fitting room I heard a saleslady in *sotto voce* excitedly telling the customers that Jayne Mansfield wasn't wearing a stitch of clothing under her dress. In no time flat the saleslady's whisper spread throughout the entire hotel, so by the time Jayne selected her new garment, a lavender suit with a collar of lynx fur, a much larger crowd had gathered (mostly men) to see whether she was or she wasn't wearing anything underneath the dress.

Well, we arrived in Dania at the Jai Alai Fronton just in time for her to present the silver cup. It was very warm inside the arena and my heart skipped several beats when a gentleman offered to help her off with her jacket. Her new outfit consisted of a skirt and a jacket, with no blouse. Seeing my frightened expression she said, "What would happen if I gave him the jacket?" Then she laughed and said, "Don't worry. I won't." And thank God, she didn't!

My husband disappeared as soon as we got there. He simply moved off to another box with the excuse that he had business to discuss with Mr. A&P or Mr. Safeway, or Mr. Grand Union or whomever.

He never did understand Jayne Mansfield. Most of the time, I thought I understood her. I figured she knew what she was doing every step of the way.

Unhappily, somewhere along the way, she lost her direction.

About a month before her horrendous and tragic death, I had supper with her in Detroit, where she was appearing in summer stock. She had a brand-new husband with her and also Mickey Hargitay who was now simply a member of her cast of actors. That night at supper, I met a completely different Jayne Mansfield. She seemed strangely remote, unhappy and thoroughly confused.

When she was killed in an automobile accident in which she was decapitated, she was already separated from the new husband I had so recently met in Detroit. Also killed with her in the car was the man she was planning to marry next.

I don't know when it was that Jayne lost her point of view. Perhaps she never had one at all. Perhaps it was only my imagination that always assured me, "She knows what she is doing!" But somehow I can't believe that was so.

I feel that somewhere along the way in Jayne's mixed-up life, the unreal became the real, and she could no longer differentiate the one from the other.

For the short time it lasted, Jayne Mansfield basked in the rays of a sometimes bright spotlight. Maybe the spotlight, bright or even dim, was all she ever wanted from life. I hope so. I'd like to think that in her short life she actually got what she wanted.

# Skelton's Farewell to Show Business

Dallas has the reputation of spawning the biggest spenders in the U.S.A. If that's true, Detroit just has to be runner-up. The Las Vegas Hilton (formerly the International) sent a United special stretch jet to transport Detroiters Sam and Alice Gruber's 150 guests to Las Vegas, the land of fun and games, for a five-day blast in honor of the Grubers' (they own the London Chop House, one of the best-known restaurants) twenty-ninth wedding anniversary.

The first night there we caught Barbra Streisand's closing, and the next night Red Skelton's opening. It was the first time in years that Skelton had played a night club.

Skelton was at his best. And Skelton, at his best, is unbeatable. You can imagine the state of shock he put his audience in when, at the end of the opening-night performance, he mournfully announced during his standing ovation: "This is my last performance in the business!"

He went on to tell how the networks had thrown him off the air. How he had been bilked by business managers. And that he was too hurt by everything to continue. He then repeated, "This is my last performance in show business."

The still-standing audience shouted: "Oh no—no!"

Then, tearfully, he walked off the stage.

It was a strange and jarring speech to hear from a man who was making his first Vegas engagement in fifteen years, and to a packed house.

I had met Red, but didn't know him very well. His "farewell to it all" speech was so moving, I rushed back to his dressing room expecting to see a broken man dissolved in tears, who for some unbelievable reason was never coming out on the stage again, not even for the second show!

Instead, there was Red sitting in a big lounge chair, with his feet up on the table, smoking an eight-foot-long cigar and smiling up a storm.

In a very shaky voice I asked, "Mr. Skelton, is this really your last time in show business? *Please* say it isn't so, sir."

"Well," he replied, "after my four weeks here, I have seven more commitments to fulfill in clubs and concerts and state fairs. I'm writing a ballet for Margot Fonteyn. Then—I'm going to make a movie for Mervyn Leroy called *The Confession.*"

That was some farewell to show business!

By now the entire Hilton management arrived en masse in Skelton's dressing room. They were more shaken up than I, afraid that he wasn't going to go on for the second performance that night.

I had read in the newspapers that after her long-time marriage to the comedian, Georgia Skelton had filed for divorce. A couple of months after that announcement, Skelton's Christmas cards still read "From Georgia and Red Skelton." I suppose he had ordered the cards earlier in the year, and so that they shouldn't be a total loss, he sent them out anyhow.

I asked the comedian about his marital status, at which point he introduced me to a Miss Toland, a very young lady who was by his side. "Her father," he said, "won several Academy Awards. Her father, you know, is Gregg Toland, the famous cinematographer."

Perhaps Miss Toland was one of the reasons Georgia was filing for divorce.

I told Jerry Lewis, who was playing Caesar's Palace at the time, about Skelton's farewell speech, and how quickly he seemed to recover in his dressing room. Jerry explained that Red is a performer who becomes every character he portrays. When he made that speech about never coming back, at that moment he believed it. Then, minutes later, in the dressing room, the real Red Skelton had already forgotten what he had said onstage about leaving show business.

Well, as they say, "You can't tell the players without a score card."

# Raquel Who?

There are very few people in show business I don't like. I've been disappointed in a few so-called friends, and there are some I no longer see by my choice or theirs, but essentially I like even those people.

Raquel Welch is the one person I really cannot abide. I don't know her well, but each meeting has been disastrous. I have always found her rude, surly and utterly uncharming—to me, at least.

I met Miss Welch first when MGM took about a hundred of us on a back-breaking press junket to Europe to view the makings of five MGM movies including *The Dirty Dozen* in London.

They also took us all to Rome where *The Biggest Bundle of Them All* was shooting on location. In this particular film there were two fine actors, Edward G. Robinson (our close personal friend) and Vittorio De Sica. Godfrey Cambridge also was a member of the cast, and so was Robert Wagner. When we arrived at the location site outside of Rome all the guys with us made a beeline for the female star of the film, Raquel Welch, whom I had never heard of until this trip. All the way from London to Rome the fellers were talking about the well-stacked Miss Welch who, for some time

228

it seems, had been gracing the covers and centerfold pages of European *Playboy* prototype magazines.

Finally it was my turn to interview this new beautiful actress. Not knowing anything about her, I asked one simple question, "How does it feel to be appearing in a movie with two great actors, Edward G. Robinson and Vittorio De Sica?" It is many years later but I can still hear her answer.

"You mean, how does it feel to have them appearing in *my* picture? I am the star." If I had done my homework and read the production notes, as I should have before we arrived, I would have realized she was telling a truth. The picture did indeed star Raquel Welch. Her name was above the title after De Sica and before Wagner and Cambridge. Eddie Robinson was billed as "guest star." After her ungracious answer she immediately walked away from me.

*The Biggest Bundle of Them All* seemed forever waiting to be released. And when, at last, it played some theatres (not too many), it bombed!

Every once in a while, if you have insomnia and are willing to stay up to watch just about anything on TV including test patterns, you might see *The Biggest Bundle of Them All* on the "late-late-late show."

It was on an Academy Award night, about a year after our first meeting, that Miss Welch was brought backstage to be interviewed along with many other stars. This is usual procedure. I think she was a presenter that night—God, you and I know she was not a nominee!

By now, I had become very aware of the name "Raquel Welch." She was becoming well known in the U.S.A. This was the year when the nationwide search was on for actresses and sex symbols to star in the movie version of Jacqueline Susann's novel *Valley of the Dolls.*

It seems every day I read somewhere that Miss Welch was cast in the film. Several days before this second meeting, the casting of *Valley of the Dolls* had been completed. I could have sworn I read that Raquel Welch had won the role of Jennifer.

Mentally forgiving her for her attitude the year before in Italy, I shoved a radio microphone into her face and said, in all sincerity, "Congratulations, Miss Welch, for nabbing the plum role of Jennifer in *Valley of the Dolls.*"

The smile vanished from her face and that old mean look came back into her eyes and around her mouth as she said, "Obviously, you don't know your business. I was offered over two hundred thousand dollars to do the role, but I turned it down. So, now Sharon Tate will play it!" Once again she walked away from me, right in the middle of my next question.

A couple of more years went by, and now Raquel Welch had become a formidable name on a theatre marquee—not exactly, however, for her acting prowess. Her publicity man, at that time, Dick Guttman, whom I trusted and thought highly of, said, "I want to get you together with Raquel. She's a great girl and I know you'll like each other if you give it a chance." Well, he had an opportunity to see for himself that there was no way I was going to get to know Raquel *well* enough to like her.

The night Frank Sinatra was to sing his "good-by forever" to show business at that marvelous benefit in Hollywood for the Motion Picture Home, I was standing outside the theatre in the Music Center gawking at the hundreds of stars walking by. It was truly one of the most exciting nights in the history of show business.

Along came Raquel on the arm of my pal, her press representative. As they walked toward me he said, "Raquel—you know Shirley Eder." Looking right through me, she walked on by. And I don't think it was because she even remembered me or our past two experiences. It was just her usual rudeness.

The next day the press agent called and said, "I

guess you're right. You two just aren't destined to become friends. I'm sorry."

Just to prove that I am not the only person to whom Raquel is rude, let me cite another incident.

The day before New Year's Eve in 1971, Raquel Welch, I'm told, showed up an hour and a half late for her manicure appointment at the beauty salon in the Beverly Hills Hotel. Margo, her manicurist (and mine too), was busy doing a woman's nails when Raquel came up to her table and said, "Are you ready for me?"

According to Margo, she answered by saying, "You are one hour and a half late, Miss Welch, but if you'll wait fifteen minutes, I'll be able to work you in."

Miss Movie Star went to a phone, made a call, and looked upset as she came back to Margo's table five minutes later repeating, "Are you ready for me *now*, Margo?"

"I told you," said the manicurist, "that it would be fifteen minutes." With that, Miss Welch turned on her heels and huffily walked out of the shop.

Realizing she had one of the shop's magazines in her hands (mean she is, a thief she is not), she came back, opened the door and flung the magazine across the waiting room, hitting the receptionist in the face,

The receptionist cried, more from shock than from pain. You can imagine what went on in that shop. Remember, it was just before New Year's Eve, and it was packed with women—and women like to talk! Okay, so am I not a woman? (Meow.)

To give Miss Welch the benefit of the doubt, I'm sure she meant only to return the magazine and did not mean to hit the receptionist. At least I don't think she did!

Just the other day I was in Hollywood, and an MGM press agent asked if I would like to interview Raquel Welch, who was starring in their movie *Kansas City Bomber*. I turned the offer down for two reasons. One, she might have belted me on sight for I have told the beauty-shop story several times on coast to coast television.

Two, she might have been extremely charming, and then there wouldn't be a single soul in show business I could really dislike. I'm often told, you can't go around liking everyone and still be successful. Thank heavens, I am saved from such a fate by Raquel Welch! I'd hate to spend the rest of my days being called "Nellie Nice." That's what a well-known female columnist had the nerve to call me to my face!

# The Manson Family

In 1970, one of the most bizarre and horrendous mass murders in the twentieth century took place in a Bel Aire, L.A. mansion. Murdered were beautiful star Sharon Tate, hair stylist Jay Sebring, Abigail Folger, Voityck Frokowsky (a Polish writer) and Steven Parent. They were brutally cut up with knives and strangled by order of an alleged madman named Charles Manson and carried out by members of his cult who called themselves the "Manson Family."

I spent a day in the Los Angeles courthouse during the trial of Manson and his followers. In the court corridors I talked with young female members of the Manson cult, who lived, along with the murderers, on a dilapidated farm called the Spahn ranch in L.A.

I had to make a telephone call, so I used the public phone booth in the corridor. When I hung up I couldn't open the door because leaning against it were several shoeless girls, who were sitting on the floor. One of them was nursing a baby. Not wanting to disturb the infant during feeding time, I waited in the booth patiently until it was finished.

I asked the girl who I thought was the mother of the child (since the infant had been feeding from her breast) how old her baby was. I was in a state of shock when she answered that it was not her child. The baby belonged to the teen-ager sitting on her right.

The one doing the nursing, I was told, had never had a child of her own; obviously, then, the baby wasn't really being fed. The real mother explained that since they were all one "family," it didn't matter who nursed the infant.

The young followers of Charles Manson, both male and female, kept roaming through the corridors. Some members of the Manson family wore hunting knives, and I'll never understand how the authorities permitted them to keep them.

When I asked one girl why she was wearing a hunting knife, she said, "It's getting pretty crazy in the city. I hitchhike down here every day and you never know who picks you up. You can't take a chance without a weapon."

Said another, "We deserve to be able to defend ourselves. And when panic strikes, a knife is a good thing to have."

Since they were all hanging around the courthouse to lend their infamous leader Charles Manson moral support, I asked the question, alluding to their pals on trial: "What about people who are not panicked and still they go out with knives, illegally enter a house and then cut up and kill total strangers who have done them absolutely no harm—can you justify that?"

A third girl shouted, "Honey, you're a reporter and you're not supposed to interject your opinions."

Then the twenty or more members of the Manson cult joined hands right there in the corridor and burst into song. In gentle childlike voices they sang out, "One is one is one."

When I asked, "What exactly did that mean 'one is one is one?' " a young man answered, "Our rules are that there are no rules. And our leaders are the babies. We follow the babies. Charles Manson followed the babies too. We take care of each other and everything."

I said then that the killers, whoever they were (since at this point there had been no pronouncement of guilt), didn't stop to think when they went to Sharon Tate's house that they weren't taking care of her and the other people inside.

A girl with blond hair and blue eyes replied, "It's love, it's love."

I insisted upon knowing what kind of love would make someone take a knife and kill. Answer: "I don't know! The country does it every day, and you're accusing *us* of murder."

I quickly explained that I was not accusing them of murder. The blond girl then said, "I don't pay any attention to what you say. I just know what I say, and what I say is truth!"

I asked another family member, "Why don't you stop copping out and start facing the real world?"

She answered, "I faced it. That's why I left it. I'm twenty-six. I went through college. I studied in Europe. I've traveled, and I say the whole world is going crazy."

She told me her name was Sandy Goode and that her father was a stockbroker. She said, "There's nothing wrong with what we do. The biggest crime today is not getting together."

I asked Sandy, because she was the most articulate, if she had children living within the Manson commune. She said she did. When I asked her who the father of her child was, she answered, "Every man! Whoever loves him—and we are all his mothers."

"Sandy, could you yourself raise a knife to kill another human being?"

She looked at me in wonder and answered, "You've got too much stuff in your head. You're on the wrong track."

I told her I was on a straight track, one on which I

thought she too had been brought up. "How did you get off that track, Sandy?" I asked.

Her answer, "I walked off, looked at it and said, 'Good-by world!' It's too crazy for me."

Our conversation ended when I said I thought there was too much killing in the world in which she lived. I still get goose bumps when I think of how a man like Manson with such a basically criminal mind could have influenced a young pretty educated woman like Sandy Goode to worship at his shrine.

Those members of the Manson cult around the courthouse were not the killers on trial with Manson, but they possibly could have been, had he bidden them to go out and do the killing the night of the Tate murders.

Inside the courtroom I kept looking at Manson, an insignificant worm of a man, on trial for sending forth killers. He was extremely short and slight of build, and he looked as though a small puff of wind could blow him away. How was this creature able to gather about him so many young people to do his maniacal bidding?

Now that Manson has been sentenced to life imprisonment, I truly hope the prison psychiatrists make a thorough study of what makes him tick. If they do, maybe they can come up with a cure by determining the cause. If the study of the mind of Manson could prevent potential Charles Mansons from committing other such terror-filled deeds, perhaps then the unfortunate Sharon Tate and those others with her will not have died in vain.

# Waiting in the Wings

In the last couple of years I have been invited to appear on many network and syndicated talk shows. This delights my immediate family simply because they can tune me out, which is something they cannot do around the house.

Thanks to Joan Rivers, who started me on the talk show route via the "Mike Douglas Show," I have since been on dozens of other shows around the country.

The one experience I will always remember is being on NBC's "Tonight Show." What the Palace was to vaudeville—that's what the "Tonight Show" is to television.

The "Tonight Show" people asked me to guest with Joan Rivers, who was subbing for Johnny Carson on the following Wednesday.

I was on a plane so fast, they couldn't possibly change their minds.

What to wear? Should I wear an evening dress? No, I decided, you're a columnist, not Zsa Zsa Gabor. Deadlines to meet in advance—meals for the family planned ahead (they could get very hungry in two days), phone calls to make around the nation asking pals to watch the "Tonight Show" on Wednesday.

Came *Der Tag.* Wednesday morning in New York. To the hair dresser—out to buy new shoes for a not so new dress—over to NBC to be questioned for hours and hours by a young "Tonight" female staffer who sat at a desk making copious notes as I told "marvelous anecdotes" with self pats on the back.

I asked, "Who's going to be on 'Tonight' tonight?"

"Tiny Tim," she said, "Jacqueline Susann, Charles Nelson Reilly, a comic named Ron Carey and possibly Zsa Zsa Gabor, who was robbed at the Waldorf last night and who just might come on to tell us how it happened."

"Super, what a line-up." Then the throat-clutching thought occurred to me: "With so many heavyweights, suppose I don't even get on?"

I asked the lady taking the notes, "Could you tell me please at what point I will be on?"

"Oh, you're the last guest," she replied, "but don't worry, Joan Rivers gets everybody in. Sometimes, with Johnny, the last guest doesn't quite make it, but never with Joanie."

Then I remembered that authors call the last ten minutes of the "Tonight Show" the "graveyard shift." And I hadn't even written a book.

"Don't worry," the staffer continued, "you'll be on about twenty minutes before closing." I took her at her word. What else could I do? Back to my hotel room to bathe and dress—make more long-distance calls announcing to America that approximately twenty minutes before 1 A.M. the next morning I would be on the "Tonight Show." Then there was the decision whether to eat before or after the show. I decided after, because it wouldn't look too good to throw up on network television.

Now is was time to go to NBC.

Into makeup with all the biggies already there— Jackie Susann, Tiny Tim, Reilly and Ron Carey. Zsa Zsa didn't show because the police wouldn't permit her to talk about the robbery—yet. Joan Rivers floated into makeup looking smashing in her new gown. "Hi," she said to one and all and floated out again. I remember thinking she gave me a special wink.

I looked great when hair dressing and makeup finished, simply because they had all that extra time to spend on me, since I was to be on last.

Finally I was escorted into a small "closed-in" room with a television set. This is called the "Green Room" where you watch the "Tonight Show" in progress and where you stay until it's time for you to go out onstage. One by one the guests were called out. One by one they went. Now the only two left in the Green Room were the comedian and myself. He paced up and down saying, "I'm glad I only have a three and one-half minute spot because I'm nervous."

I joked a lot (on the square) telling him when he got on to hurry up so I could get my chance.

Charles Nelson Reilly was so good he was held over an extra five minutes. Tiny Tim was such a smash, he sang an extra song. Jackie Susann, always a good talker, was better than ever and stayed on for an extra segment. Joan Rivers was in great funny form so she ad-libbed a lot. It was now twenty minutes before one A.M. and Ron Carey's turn. He went on—and on—and on. His allotted three-and-a-half minutes became ten.

I looked at my watch—only ten minutes before the show goes off the air and no one had come to fetch me from the Green Room, which by now had turned into a jail cell for me, and I was the lifer who had been forgotten.

Out I marched, uninvited, into the wings in time to see the producers giving the comedian the wind-up signal, which they had been doing for some seven minutes.

Standing in the wings, I heard Joan Rivers say on the air, "We won't have time for Shirley Eder, but maybe we can get her to come back on Friday night."

My jail sentence changed from life imprisonment to the electric chair.

Suddenly, Joan called my name and said, "Come on out, Shirley, just to say good night." There I was in front of Mr. and Mrs. America where, in less than five minutes, I managed to shout all over the United States, who was doing what to whom, praying the people I talked about would not be watching. I hadn't planned to gossip, but there was no time for anecdotes.

From that night on I watch the "Tonight Show" with much more compassion for the guests—and, believe me, so should you!

It's a rough go that first time around. Almost immediately after that show there was a change of producer and most of the staff. Honest, I had nothing to do with it. How could I, in less than five minutes?

# The Fall of a Giant

One night during the last year of his life Walter Winchell was at Chasen's restaurant in Beverly Hills, sitting all by himself in the middle booth on the right-hand side of the restaurant. That night I received a compliment from him I will remember. A compliment from Walter Winchell to a reporter was tantamount to an actor being presented with an Academy Award.

Because he was sitting alone (although by choice), I somehow felt that perhaps he'd like just one person to come over and say "Hi, Walter." Whether he did or he didn't, I went over to his table, put my hand out, and said, "Walter Winchell, I don't know if you remember me—I'm Shirley Eder."

After inviting me to sit down, he said, "Of course I remember you, Shirley. What's more, I've been following your career as a columnist and you are doing a fine job."

Wow! Coming from the man who invented the gossip column (after Samuel Pepys), this indeed was praise.

Years before, I just happened to be on the scene at the Stork Club in New York the night Walter Winchell's column empire began to tumble down.

241

For lots of years men of power tried unsuccessfully to dethrone Mr. Winchell. It took an incident in which he really was an innocent bystander to finally do it.

My husband and I after threatre were in the Cub Room of the famous Stork Club. Sherman Billingsley, the owner, kept a red rope up at the door of the main room admitting mostly only the affluent and/or influential people of the world. More often than not, the stern maitre d' in charge would turn those he did not know personally away by saying, "You cannot come in without a reservation." And that was not true. The red rope was a brilliant idea because everyone wants "in" where it's tough to get in!

The Cub Room was the inner sanctum for Billingsley's chosen patrons. There was never a night when the place wasn't loaded with visiting movie stars from Hollywood, top political figures, and the rich, famous and infamous from all walks of life.

Edward and I were very young at the time. I don't know how we made it past the first red rope, much less the second, into the Cub Room. But for some reason Sherman Billingsley liked us and bestowed upon us some of the same favors as he did on his important guests. We had dinner there often on Sunday nights. Sometimes there would be no check. Often he gave me a bottle of the famous Stork Club Sortilege perfume. And just as often a bottle of imported French champagne would arrive at our table with the message "Compliments of Mr. Billingsley." If we received such favors, you can imagine what the VIPs got.

Walter Winchell used the Stork Club as his extra office. Through numerous mentions in his column, Billingsley's Stork Club became the most important night club in New York.

At some point every evening Winchell would show up and sit at Table 50, the first table you saw as you came into the Cub Room. At least a half a dozen people sat there with him, and dozens more would come over to whisper items and stories into his ear, all courting his favor. There was always a telephone at Mr. Winchell's table. There, he would receive calls from J. Edgar Hoover, Bob Hope or maybe even from the President of the United States.

Although I was not yet writing for newspapers I did have radio shows and, later, TV shows in New York. Looking back on the scene in retrospect, I should have been ashamed of having been so delighted to be a part of such snobbery. Yet it was fun to be around what was called "Café Society." Today such a group is categorized in *Women's Wear Daily* as the "B.P." (Beautiful People) set or the "Cat Pack."

Actually, it was the snob appeal that made the Cub Room so successful.

One night in the Cub Room we witnessed the beginning of the downfall of Walter Winchell's career. This night, the room was not too crowded. Walter Winchell was not sitting at his usual table. Instead, he was at a small table next to the door. We saw Sherman Billingsley come into the room looking pale and angry. He stopped at Walter's table to whisper something into his ear, then he turned and left the room.

Josephine Baker, the internationally famous black singer who had exiled herself years before to Paris, arrived at the Cub Room with a party of people. We saw Winchell greet her, then leave the club, which was not unusual because Winchell never stayed in one club the whole evening.

I remember the service was not particularly good on this night, and we waited a long time for our food, and we noticed that Josephine Baker and her party were not served immediately. We also realized that Billingsley never came back into the room. This was unusual!

Back in the 1950s black people, no matter how famous, were not exactly welcomed in places like the Stork Club. And one always heard rumors about Sherman Billingsley's thorough dislike for all minorities.

But in New York, if that was so, there wasn't much he could do about barring prominent people of the Jewish faith from his club. What's more, the man who made the Stork Club world-famous, Walter Winchell, was himself a Jew.

Back to Josephine Baker: Not too long after she and her party arrived, Miss Baker got up from her table and left the room. She was gone for some time. When she returned, there was much whispering and conferring in her party. Then they all got up and left.

We knew there was something happening. We didn't know what it was, but we were sure that some kind of trouble was abrewin'. Miss Baker and party certainly did not receive Billingsley's usual VIP treatment—but neither were they ignored by the captain or the waiters. We left soon after.

Again I want to point out the fact that Walter Winchell had left the club shortly after Miss Baker's arrival.

When we got back to our apartment, I turned on the radio to listen to Barry Gray, who hosted a popular late-night talk show.

Sure enough, there on Barry's show, talking excitedly, was Josephine Baker and a top official from the NAACP, both condemning the Stork Club for its ill treatment of her and both vehemently berating Walter Winchell for not coming to her aid when he saw how badly she was being treated.

I was furious, not with the things they had to say about Sherman Billingsley because they were obviously true, but hearing them say that Walter Winchell witnessed her humiliation made me really angry. I don't discount the fact that he may have left knowing there could be trouble after Billingsley came to see him. But he honestly played no active part in whatever humiliation Miss Baker and party may have been subjected to that night.

This was the beginning of national fame for Barry Gray and the beginning of the end for Walter Win-

chell as the number-one kingmaker and kingbreaker.
Every important person who hated Winchell and had
tried in vain to destroy him through the years jumped
on the "Let's Kick Winchell" band wagon. For many
weeks after, Winchell's enemies showed up on Barry
Gray's popular program to reveal all the terrible things
they either knew or made up about the columnist. He
was denounced as a racist by everyone including New
York *Daily News* columnist Ed Sullivan, who had a
long-time feud going with Winchell.

During his career, Winchell had definitely hurt people; on the other hand, he had also helped just as
many to success and fame. If Winchell praised a performer, that performer's career was made.

I hold no brief for many of the things Walter Winchell said and did. But this time I was witness to what
seemed to me trumped-up accusations against the
man.

Winchell devoted subsequent columns to denying
the accusations—but no one seemed to listen. He had
had a long, long run as the number-one newsman, but
his reign was coming to an end. The timing of the
Josephine Baker-Winchell fracas was right as far as
his enemies were concerned. It was post-World War
II and the world was ready for all sorts of changes.

Several months after the Winchell-Baker holocaust
(which had not yet subsided), I was lunching with
Adele Haupt, a friend who said she had been taking
French reading courses. I didn't pay much attention,
until from out of nowhere she said that she had been
looking through some books in a little shop that spe-
cialized in books written in French. Seems she came
across an autobiography written many years before by
Josephine Baker, which had been published in Paris.

In it she spoke of the inhumanities of the Jewish
landlords in Harlem and she blasted the New York
Jews.

When we left the restaurant, I asked her to take me
immediately to the store where she had seen it. Sure

enough, it was still there. So I bought this out-of-print book for two dollars, then I took it to a French-American Adele knew, and word for word he translated the chapter in which Josephine Baker, who was now damning Walter Winchell for being a racist and anti-black, displayed overt anti-Semitism. It was right there in print.

It took many hours for the translation and the copying of it to be completed, and I didn't get home until late that evening. What started out to be lunch with a friend turned into a *cause célèbre*.

From home, I called all over town looking for Walter Winchell, hoping that what I had learned from Josephine Baker's autobiography would give him at least some ammunition to defend himself against her attack.

I knew he stayed at the St. Moritz Hotel when he was in New York, but when I called he wasn't in. I tried many of his familiar haunts, but no one had seen him that night. I finally got in touch with Roy Cohn whom I knew was a close friend of Walter's. Roy told me to sit tight and said he'd try and track him down.

When my husband went to sleep, I debated whether or not I should go to bed or stay fully clothed just in case Mr. Winchell called and wanted to see me.

At midnight the call came from Roy Cohn saying, "Walter wants you to meet him in a private office in the Stork Club at 1 A.M. Can you come? If you can, please bring the book and the translation with you."

I was afraid to wake my husband for fear he would tell me I was crazy and wouldn't let me go. By now, I felt like Mata Hari and I was playing it to the hilt.

So-o-o-o, at 12:45, I very quietly closed the apartment door behind me, went down in the elevator and out the front door. I admit I was ashamed to be leaving the building by myself at that hour. I was convinced that the doorman would think I was sneaking out on my husband, which I was, but not for the reason he would think.

At 1 A.M. on the dot, I arrived at the Stork Club. Roy Cohn was waiting behind the red rope to whisk me up to the private office where the high priest of the Fourth Estate was waiting to see me.

Another man was there with Walter. I think he was a lawyer. Walter, Roy and he thoroughly read the translation, then Winchell asked if he could keep both the book and the translation. I was so thrilled to be part of this post-midnight caper, I didn't even ask for the money it cost to get the book translated.

Walter Winchell threw his arms around me and said, "What you have given me may or may not do me any good. But whether or not it does, I'll never forget the fact that you wanted to help me."

Around three o'clock in the morning, I sneaked back into the apartment worried that this escapade might possibly mean the end of my marriage. Fortunately, as I came into the bedroom, I heard Edward snoring and knew that I was home safe. When I told him about it the next morning at breakfast, he couldn't believe the whole episode and said, "It's a good thing I didn't get up before you came home. If I had, the door would have been double locked from the inside."

Twenty-four hours later, in his column in the New York *Daily Mirror* Winchell used the translation of the entire chapter. But at this point, unfortunately, not too many people cared.

Walter Winchell from time to time used to put my name in his column. Once he gave me an "orchid" (his highest accolade) for a radio show I had. However, from that night of the meeting to the day he stopped writing his column, Walter Winchell never again mentioned my name in print.

Often I thought of what he said to me the night I brought him the translation of Josephine Baker's autobiography: "I'll never forget the fact that you wanted to help me!"

Incidentally, it was Winchell's many columns of praise about Josephine Baker years before the Stork Club incident which helped to make her the "toast of New York."

Several years after we moved to Detroit, Josephine Baker appeared · in a variety show at the Shubert Theatre. There, over lunch when I interviewed her, I asked why she had wanted to hurt Walter Winchell, and I told her I had been at the Stork Club that night.

Miss Baker said that day that she was very sorry about the whole affair. She realized now that she had been used as a pawn in the matter, and Walter had done nothing to hurt her. She also said she had written many letters of apology to Mr. Winchell but had never received an answer. Miss Baker also told me that she realized that it had been Walter Winchell who was responsible for her success in America, saying that before he wrote about her as a performer, her name meant nothing in this country.

The irreparable damage to Walter Winchell's career had already been done and I wasn't about to interfere again by trying to get in touch with him to relay what she told me in Detroit.

Walter Winchell is dead, and l'affaire Baker-Winchell-Stork Club is now an incident which only a few of us remember.

# Dilly Deli

Nate 'n' Al's, a delicatessen in Beverly Hills, shows no preference to movie stars, since they make up at least half of the steady patrons. There are absolutely no reservations, so standing in line, right next to you, waiting for a table could be Milton Berle, Greer Garson with her multimillionaire oilman husband, Buddy Fogelson, Rock Hudson or even movie mogul Jack Warner.

When Barbara Stanwyck was ill (she's extremely well now) at St. John's Hospital in 1971, I decided she should have the panacea for all ills—chicken soup.

Figuring Nate 'n' Al's chicken soup would be the most likely to taste homemade, I was willing to stand in line to get some at the take-out counter. At that counter, at all times of the day and night, people are lined up holding numbers in their hands.

While I was waiting to pick up the chicken soup to take to Barbara, I saw Groucho Marx standing next to me holding the number 70. My number was 68. Since the countermen were only up to number 50, Groucho, who didn't know me, asked if I would hold his numbered card for him while he went next door to the drugstore for a few minutes, just in case his number was called while he was gone. When he returned, they still were nowhere near his 70.

"You won't believe this," said Groucho, "but I'm standing on line all this time waiting for three bagels! What's more, this is the first time—the very first time —I have ever bought a bagel in my life!"

I told him I couldn't quite believe that any one of Minnie's boys (Minnie Marx) had never eaten a bagel.

"Oh," he said, "I've *eaten* bagels plenty of times, but I never purchased one before. My various wives and housekeepers always bought them for me."

I mumbled something about it being kind of silly to stand in line all that time for just three bagels.

"You're right," he continued, "but I ate some up at Frank's house last night and they were so good that when I learned they came from Nate 'n' Al's, I decided to come here and buy some for myself."

I knew who he meant by "Frank," and I also knew he wanted me to ask "Frank who?" I did, and of course he replied, "Frank Sinatra!"

Finally, Groucho's tiny package was ready. "Who'd believe," he said, shaking his head, "I'd stand in line for forty-five minutes waiting for a thirty-cent package?"

All I kept thinking was "Say the magic woid, Groucho, and the bagels will be yours."

All delicatessen countermen have something in common: They are all comedians! As Groucho was leaving Nate 'n' Al's, the counterman shouted, "Hey, Groucho, Enjoy! Enjoy the bagels, but don't go swimming after you eat one!"

I wrote about the bagel incident in my syndicated newspaper column, and not, at the time, having Groucho's address, I sent a copy to "Groucho Marx, c/o Nate 'n' Al's, Beverly Drive, Beverly Hills, California—HOLD FOR ARRIVAL." He must have "arrived" the very next day, because less than a week later I received a letter from Groucho saying, "I especially liked picking up my mail at Nate 'n' Al's. And I'm arranging for the post office to send all my mail there from now on—that way I won't have always to read the menu, which hasn't been changed since the place opened."

Also in the letter, Groucho talked about going on one of the midnight talk shows simply because there was a young actress he was crazy about and she was going on the show with him. He wrote: "She's been in show business for years, but is terrified of doing a talk show and I thought it would be a good experience for her." This led me to wonder what else she was experiencing with that fabulous funny man with the cigar, the lecherous walk and the three bagels.

# La Dietrich

It was no surprise to me that Marlene Dietrich wasn't all that nice to the press when CBS decided to have a big press hoopla to greet her on her arrival in New York last January in conjunction with her first TV special (on CBS, of course), produced in England by Alexander Cohen.

In February of 1971 I was invited to the Playboy Hotel in Miami Beach, along with several other columnists, to attend a press conference and opening of the great Dietrich.

At the conference Miss Dietrich was pretty much noncommunicative and mumbled most of her answers. It was evident then that she was either scared or bored with all of us.

The press party didn't last too long, and I managed to get a few (very few) words alone with her. We were told that no one was permitted to watch Marlene rehearse her act, which is understandable. However, I decided to somehow sneak in and catch her rehearsal. Soooo—

Someone backstage told me that several times during music breaks, Marlene ordered room service for her crew. An imaginative Playboy Hotel executive suggested that I hop into a bunny outfit and go in as an employee. He was either kidding or knew the flattery would get him everywhere. Alas—I don't have the figure to be a Playboy bunny. But his idea begat another.

I decided to borrow a regular waitress uniform and go into the rehearsal carrying a tray of coffee cups. I waited and waited, hoping the star would order from room service. When she didn't, I finally went in anyway, carrying a couple of cups. She was much too busy to even notice as I walked to the back of the room and sat down.

Dietrich was the perfectionist I knew she would be, even in rehearsing—over and over again—her sensational bows. At one point, she called up to her lighting man and said, "I vant more light, all the bright lights you can give me." Most lady stage stars past the age of thirty ask for pale pinks. Not Marlene.

Over and over again, she sang her numbers for the light man. Most performers, if they have done the act before, rehearse for just a couple of hours before the opening. Marlene rehearsed three whole days. Her contract calls for sixteen hours' rehearsal time with full orchestra. She said, "The success of my performance depends on beauty in all departments. Not only the way I look and zound, but alzo the vay the musicians look and zound."

I know that one time in Montreal one of her ten violinists wore short socks during a performance. At the end of the show she turned to him and said, "The next performance you vill vear long socks, please!" And he did!

I was fascinated watching her turn to listen to each section of the large orchestra as they rehearsed. And when she finished a dramatic song, she called to the man up in the booth and said, "I vant it to go completely dark at the end. I vill signal you by throwing my head back—bung, like this (throwing her blond head back), and the lights go out. Then ve—you and

I—vill count one, two, three, four, five, six, and your lights go up again—and I bow."

I was impressed by her interest in detail and knowledge. She even called the management who would present her with flowers onstage opening night to tell them to make sure it was a nosegay of varied flowers on doilies with little ribbons hanging from the stems. "No prickles and no thorns, please" was her request. Obviously, Miss Dietrich had been "stuck" before.

It was almost time for the real waitresses and waiters to come in to set tables for the first show, so I stole out the back door. Marlene continued to rehearse without ever knowing I was there.

Under the spell of something extraordinary called the "Dietrich mystique," everyone thought the opening was marvelous.

Marlene had told the publicity department of the Playboy Hotel that after the show they could bring several executives of Playboy, Inc., and some key press people backstage. When the nine or ten of us showed up, we were asked by her male secretary to stand away from the dressing-room door, which we did.

Several minutes later he came out of the dressing room and asked us all to wait in another part of the hall.

A few minutes after that, we were asked to walk through a door to wait on the other side. His star did not like to feel crowded. The visiting VIPs and press walked out that door—and kept right on walking. Someone in a mock German accent said, "Dis vay to the ovens!"

If the lady had changed her mind about seeing her guests, so had the guests changed their mind about seeing her. However, she was strangely fascinating.

I asked a couple of female stars who were as important on the Paramount lot when Dietrich was there as a reigning star if she had been different during those golden years. One of them, a major star still, replied, "How should I know; she never deigned to even speak to me during all our years on the same lot!"

# But Not This Time, Cary Grant

It wasn't easy to get to Cary Grant. But through writer-producer Stanley Shapiro, who had at the time scripted Cary's hit picture *Operation Petticoat* and the Doris Day-Rock Hudson starrer *Pillow Talk*, I managed to meet "THE MAN." Stanley, a close friend of Cary's, made arrangements for me to visit with Grant in his office bungalow on the Universal lot.

By no means was I going to see Cary Grant with my face hanging out *au naturel.* So, on that particular day, I went to the "Wagon Train" set, where Barbara Stanwyck was starring in an episode, and got her to ask her makeup man to try to make me look glamorous.

Cary Grant is one actor who creates as much excitement with his peers as he does with the rest of us. The cast working with Barbara was thrilled about my upcoming interview, and made me promise to come back right after to report everything he said and did.

Anyone who visited a "Wagon Train" set knows that because of the many horses used in the series, the smell around there was "Manure Number 5."

Barbara said, "You can't visit Cary Grant smelling like that," so she doused me with the perfume she

uses, Tuvach's Jungle Gardenia. Just as I was about
to depart for the big date, I flung over my shoulder
to all within earshot: "I'll be back when I've finished
with Mr. Grant, but don't expect me too soon!"

Barbara's reply: "Wanna bet you'll be back in fifteen
minutes?"

I arrived at Mr. Grant's studio bungalow with a
face looking like, I hoped, a combination of Elizabeth
Taylor's and Ava Gardner's. At least that's the way
the makeup man *should* have made me look. Hollywood makeup men have been known to accomplish
the impossible, so don't laugh.

I gave the secretary in the outer office my name.
She said, "Oh, Miss Eder, Mr. Grant is waiting for
you." Cary Grant was waiting for *me!!*

The inner door opened and there he stood—looking
exactly like Cary Grant! My God, what a beautiful
man he truly is! He put his hand out to shake mine.
Then, he took me into his office living room. Sitting
on a couch was Milton Green, the photographer who
had helped Marilyn Monroe to fame. I was disappointed to see someone else there—I thought I was
going to have Cary Grant all to myself.

Cary asked, "Do you like music?"

When I answered, "Yes," he pushed a button and in
stereo from out of the woodwork came beautiful
strains of classical music. I thought to myself, "I'm
not alive. I'm in another world and I'm spending eter-
nity with Cary Grant."

Then he asked, "Would you like a cup of tea?"

He might as well have been asking, "Would you like
to elope?" because that's the way he made it sound.
He brewed the tea himself. Cary Grant was brew-
ing tea for me!

After he seated me in a chair in front of his desk,
he sat down behind it. I remember saying, "Mr. Grant,
even if we finish this interview in five minutes, would
you let me stay in your outer office for fifty-five min-

utes more?" I repeated Barbara Stanwyck's parting words "You'll be back in fifteen minutes."

He must have thought this pretty funny, because he honest to goodness chuckled from somewhere down deep. He assured me that we would indeed talk together for an hour.

Before I could think of a thing to say, he looked across the desk into my eyes and said, "Now, tell me about yourself."

There I was telling Cary Grant all about me. Something was wrong with the interview, but I wasn't about to change a second of it! I don't remember too much of what I said except I did make my children much, much younger than they really were. I think at the time my son was five and my daughter eleven, but I can still hear myself saying they were two and three years of age. It didn't matter that Cary Grant was older than I, I wanted to be so young for him.

We talked and talked and talked. I didn't write a word down. I just listened to his voice. As I looked across at him—he wasn't sitting in a chair behind a desk. No sireeee. He was dressed in shining silver armor sitting astride a white horse. I know he was saying other things, but in my mind I kept hearing him say, "You will come away with me, won't you?" "Oh, the tricks the mind can play." (Lyrics by Larry Hart.)

The music, the tea (what was in that tea?), the soft lights—all were influential in leading me to believe this was not an interview but a "special happening" between a man and a woman.

A ringing telephone brought me back to reality, and I looked at my watch. I had been sitting there trancelike for almost two hours. I didn't want to go, but I knew the time had come. Only after the phone rang did I remember there was a third person in the room. I had forgotten all about Milton Green who was sitting on the couch the entire time.

Before I said good-by I said, "You know, Mr. Grant, always when I come home from Hollywood and have met or interviewed the great male superstars of the screen, I'm so glad to get back to my husband that I stop in at the Beverly Hills Hotel's men's shop and buy him a present. That's how happy I am to get back to him."

He said, "That's the nicest thing I ever heard. That's really nice."

I answered: "But not this time, Cary Grant!"

I went back to that "Wagon Train" set in a daze. The whole cast gathered around to hear what Cary Grant had to say. I didn't want to touch any of them because they looked so bedraggled in their "Wagon Train" costumes—especially my friend Barbara Stanwyck, who was portraying a white woman who had been captured by the Indians. Hadn't I just come from the neatest, cleanest, handsomest man in the world?

I remember going back to the Beverly Hills Hotel and calling Ginger Rogers, who at several different times, had gone steady with Cary Grant. At this point in her life, she had only recently been married to Bill Marshall. I said on the phone, "Ginger, you must have been out of your mind. Why didn't you marry Cary Grant? What's the matter with you?"

Her reply to me from the other end was "Yes, it is a nice day, Shirley."

"Waddaya mean nice day? I was with him! He's marvelous! If you could have, you should-have married him. I don't understand you!"

She said, "Yes, we'll meet you for dinner at seven-thirty."

Only then did I realize that her new husband must have been standing close by. You see, my husband wasn't jealous because there was no way an alliance between Cary Grant and this reporter could become a reality.

With Ginger—well, that was different.

# More About Cary Grant

After that first long interview with Cary Grant, I was actually bewitched. I drove everyone around me nuts by the telling and the retelling of how he even made me tea. At home, the name "Cary Grant" was as much in usage at our dinner table as were the names of my children or "Pass the salt." Edward approved of my relationship with Mr. Grant, secure in the knowledge that it was totally one-sided—mine!

About two months later, I was back on the West Coast. Mitzi Gaynor was making a movie on the Universal lot. I called and asked if I could come out and have lunch with her. She said, "Sure, we'll have it brought to my dressing room. When I'm working I never eat in the commissary."

In spite of her protest about never eating in the commissary while she was working, I coerced her into doing it just this one time. You see, I knew that's where Cary Grant ate his lunch every day.

I also knew that Cary thought Mitzi was something pretty special because during our interview he told me he had just seen her perform in Las Vegas and he thought she was just great.

Mitzi insisted on knowing why I had to eat in the

commissary. And this is what I told her: "First, I'm going to have my hair set, then buy extra long eyelashes. And then I am going to pack a bag which I will put under the table in the commissary. I want to be ready when Cary Grant walks in and sees me sitting there, because I know he's going to ask me to elope with him. And I have Edward's permission because he can understand any woman running off with Cary Grant!"

Mitzi, after hearing that speech, agreed to lunch in the commissary.

Well, we sat there for about a half hour—no Cary Grant. Mitzi kept looking at her watch saying, "I have to go back to work. You know I'm in the middle of a picture. Why can't you sit here alone and order some dessert?"

That kind of courage I don't have. Just as Mitzi asked for the check—I saw him! There he stood—in the doorway! He looked as if he was stepping off the screen into my life. Everyone else in the commissary must have felt the same way. He's the only actor who causes every other actor and actress to turn around to look at him when he comes into a room.

I was facing the door. Mitzi sat beside me. Cary looked over and smiled, which made me exclaim, "He sees me! He sees me! He's coming toward the table. When I leave with Cary Grant, call Edward and tell him it happened."

Cary made a direct beeline for our table. I kept thinking, "He remembers me. He *does* remember me."

As I was about to put my arms out to him, he threw his arms around Mitzi, hugged her tight and said, "You're the most talented girl I know. When are we going to dance together again? When are you going to teach me some of those new dances?"

He went on at length talking only to Mitzi, who finally said, "You know Shirley Eder, don't you?"

Barely glancing my way, he said, "Yes, how do you do?" Then he went on raving to Mitzi about Mitzi.

Well, sir, I went home and wrote a column telling it like it was—even the part about having my bag packed, etc., etc. Someone sent that column to Cary. One day when I came into the studio in Detroit to do a television show, Marie, the switchboard operator, said, "A Mr. Grant has been calling you from Los Angeles."

My mother's maiden name is Grant and I wondered if we had any relatives in Los Angeles. The flash! "Could it be—Cary Grant?!!?"

"No-o-o-o, Cary Grant wouldn't be calling me."

Marie said, "Whoever it is, he said he would call back at three o'clock." So I just sat me down at the telephone in the reception room of WJBK for forty-five minutes—until the clock struck three.

In the meantime, word had gotten around the station that maybe Cary Grant was going to call Shirley Eder. Did I ever have plenty of company in the reception room? Every secretary and several company executives hung around making small talk.

At three o'clock, a red light on her switchboard lit up and Marie shouted, "It's for you, Shirley, it's for you from Hollywood." She plugged me in. It was such a faint connection I'm sure every other office was also plugged in on the call.

That familiar voice on the other end said, "Shirley, this is Cary." Knowing everybody was listening, I casually said, "Cary, how are you?"

Boy, was I playing it cool, considering that inside I was shaking. He said, "This connection is not very clear. Is there anyone else on your line?"

I assured him that there couldn't be anything wrong on our end, knowing damn well the reason for the bad connection.

He said, "I'm in the middle of making out my income tax, and I was feeling pretty low until someone put your column on my desk, the one in which you told the story of how you and Mitzi came to the commissary for lunch. Shirley," he laughed, "how could I have ignored you? How could I have done anything like that to you? Obviously, I just didn't see you. Can I ever make it up to you? I'm coming right there to get you."

I hoped everyone, but everyone, was listening in!

From that day on Cary and I became good friends. He still calls me from time to time—sometimes at home, sometimes at the paper; sometimes I receive a message from my service saying that he called just to say "Hello."

Once in recent years, my husband and I were checking in at the Diplomat Hotel in Hollywood, Florida. We had come down for the Jackie Gleason Pro-Am Golf Tournament. It was Florida's busy season and dozens of harried people waiting for rooms were lined up at the registration desk. When we finally reached the desk the clerk told us that our rooms were not ready, and we'd just have to wait. Nobody likes to come from a cold to a tropical climate, swathed in winter clothing, to be told "You can't get into your rooms." No matter how air-conditioned the lobby is, it's still plenty hot in your snow-type outer garments.

My husband, annoyed by the situation, went out to see about having the bags brought in and the rented car garaged. I walked away from the desk. Several minutes later, the desk clerk, with a phone in hand, shouted, "Is there a Shirley Eder here?"

Thoroughly irked with having to summon me, the clerk said, "There's a long-distance call for you."

Well, I couldn't take a long-distance call over that crowded desk so I requested him to please ask who was calling so that I could call whoever it was back when we finally got to our rooms. In a new respectful tone, the reception clerk exclaimed, "It's Cary Grant!"

I wasn't about to miss this call. I asked if there was a phone somewhere where I could talk to Mr. Grant. The clerk pointed to a white house phone on the other side of the lobby.

You may have heard of "Arnie's army" (Arnold Palmer). Well, his is nothing compared to "Shirley's army that day." After the clerk shouted out the name "Cary Grant," a mob then followed me over to the white phone.

Cary said that he had called me in Detroit, and the service told him where I was. I explained that we were still in the lobby and not able to get into our rooms. He thought the situation terrible (which it was), and said that if we needed a place to stay, he had a friend with a beautiful apartment in Miami Beach, and he was sure his friend would be happy to turn it over to us.

I assured him that it wouldn't be necessary because eventually we would get our rooms. Cary, genuinely worried, said, "Now you take my phone number, and if you have trouble, just call me and I'll see that you have a place to stay."

I fumbled for a pencil and paper and began to repeat his number digit by digit until I noticed dozens of pencils and pieces of paper taking the number down, right along with me. Fortunately, I became aware of the situation by the fourth digit. The last three I scribbled in code. When I hung up I saw my husband rushing toward me. Seeing me in the middle of a crowd he thought I'd had an accident.

I don't know if it was Cary's call or a mere coincidence, but we were immediately informed the rooms were vacant and ready now for occupancy.

Ten minutes after we checked in, the phone rang. A man on the other end said he was Norman Zeiler, a friend of Cary Grant's. He was calling from New York to say that Cary had called him from California to tell him of our plight and to ask if we could use his apartment in Miami Beach.

My husband hearing the name "Norman Zeiler" took the phone from me. It turned out they had been gin-playing buddies years before, when we lived in New York. Norman told Edward that Cary must have really liked us because he was so concerned about our having a place to sleep that night. Said Norman, "My friend Cary, believe me, would not do this for just anyone. He must think a lot of you."

Zeiler went on to say he would be in Miami several days later and made a date to take us to dinner when he arrived.

No sooner had he hung up when the phone rang again. A woman said that she was Mrs. Norman Zeiler and that Cary had called to ask her to invite us to stay in their apartment. We explained that we were already settled in our rooms, but that we deeply appreciated the invitation from both her and her husband. When I asked where she was calling from, she answered, "Oh, from my apartment right here in Miami Beach."

Can you imagine people being nice enough to invite strangers to move in with them because a friend asked them to? This only proves what I have always known: My Cary Grant can move mountains.

We had dinner with the Zeilers at their country club a few days later, and we had a big laugh over the coincidence of our husbands having known each other. Norman said there is nothing Cary Grant won't do for a friend.

Maybe I didn't get to elope with my hero, but it's almost as satisfying to be able to call him "friend." I said *almost!*

# "Operation Bob Hope"

Toward the end of November 1972 I picked up the
phone to hear Bob Hope's press agent Frank Liberman
say, "Well, have you finished packing to go on Bob's
last Christmas trip to Thailand and Vietnam? And
Bob wants to know why he hasn't heard from you
about it." Several months before, when Bob and Dolores Hope were in Detroit, Bob mentioned my going
with him on this year's Christmas visit, to Asia. But
since I never heard from him again on the subject, I
thought he was kidding and forgot all about it.

Well, he wasn't kidding. I learned that when Bob
Hope says something, he means it! Immediately, I
rushed out to take all the necessary shots in both but-
tocks and both arms ("ouch").

What an experience it was visiting army, marine,
Seabee and naval bases with "Operation Bob Hope!"
Unless you have been there to see for yourself, there
is no way you can possibly imagine just how important
those Christmas visits were to thousands of guys in
uniform who could not be home with loved ones at
Christmastime.

At every base, boys would arrive at midnight the
night before Bob's expected arrival just to stake out a

place on the hard ground, even though the show might not be starting until after lunch the next day.

At Nam Phong, Thailand, the twenty-five hundred Marines stationed at this dusty desolate spot proved that they can really take it. In the 100-degree temperature (and it was winter in Thailand), the men built for themselves whatever small comforts they had such as showers with cold water only and rough wood planks covering the ground in their tents. Nam Phong is the Air Force Task Force Delta Marine Base that had three gun squadrons, two F-4 squads and six Intruder squadrons; it was the support air operation for all of Southeast Asia. The base was surrounded by rice paddies and jungle and was easily reached for sneak attacks, and throughout the performance, we saw many of the men patrolling the surrounding jungle area, some with vicious dogs.

Nam Phong is 255 miles from Bangkok. There is no such thing as TV, only an occasional movie, and the men have no place to go on short leaves. So you can imagine what seeing Hope, Fran Jeffries, Lola Falana, eight beauty-contest winners and Redd Foxx meant to them.

While we were there I walked around questioning at least three hundred noncom Marines who, to a man, agreed with the President on the stepped-up bombings. The President's bombing edict was handed down just about the time we arrived in Thailand. All of us, including Bob, thought we would arrive as peace was declared, instead of the renewed fighting.

A Marine pilot who had lost his brother and three of his flying buddies in recent bombings told me that every time there was a "cease fire," it gave the enemy time to regroup and to ambush them when the cease fire was lifted. "I don't believe," he said, "there should be another cease fire until there is a signed peace. I've lost too many friends for me to give the enemy time to find new hiding places to kill me or someone else close to me."

Redd Foxx was delighted when we disembarked from the C141 cargo plane, on which we flew every place. The first thing we saw was a tank with a sign on top that read: "We Deal in Fine Junk, Too. Welcome Redd Foxx and Sanford and Son." Said Redd, "I had to come all this way to really know what I'm worth to NBC." You can bet when he got back to the States, he upped the ante for his talents. Redd has no agents or business managers. He handles all of his own deals.

To read about it is one thing, but to be right there at UDORN when an American F-4 returns to base after its two-man crew has just shot down a MIG . . . is something else. The pilot was doused in champagne just like a winning World Series player.

Later that day, after the excitement of victory died down, I asked the pilot if, while he was up there, he thought about the fact that he was possibly killing another human being. He replied, "No, when you are up there and see a MIG coming at you, it's either the MIG or you. You're fighting for your own life at the time. But later, like now, you do think about the guy in the other plane, and hope like hell he got out of it okay. What's more, as you sit around with the guys over a beer, you wish the guy in that MIG was here having a beer with you, so you could talk it over together."

As we were en route to Singapore on board our home-away-from-home, the C141 luxuryless cargo plane, which was stripped of everything to make way for the necessary seats—and I mean stripped of *everything*, including coverings for the pipes in the roof of the plane—I had time to reflect on what in my opinion was the most dangerous part of our tour.

Sure, we were in danger zones like Saigon. When we got back in the plane to leave there, we shot up into the sky like a bat out of hell because of the possibility of anti-aircraft missiles reaching us once we went beyond the periphery of our own protective air power.

But we were in greater danger when "Operation Bob Hope" was given time off in Bangkok to shop! Now that was *really* scary. All eighty-five of us, which included the camera crew, cast, writers, stars and press, ran around like crazy people, bargaining, buying and bluffing about prices.

Back in the U.S.A. we normally exaggerate the prices when we brag about purchases to friends. Over in Bangkok the heroes in our group were those who bought the cheapest. I.e., if you bought a ring for eight bucks, Lola Falana or Miss World would swear she got the same ring for two dollars less.

Miss Norway and several of those gorgeous beauty-contest winners traveling with Operation Hope, came down with fatigue, all kinds of flu bugs, stomach bugs and heat prostration, yet nothing was more hazardous on the trip than trying to cross a street in Bangkok on foot.

Instead of that old gag "Why does a chicken cross the road?" we asked, "Why does a member of the Bob Hope group cross the road?" Answer: Because someone said, "It's cheaper on the other side!"

I'm told a traffic expert from Germany was brought to Bangkok to survey the situation and to advise the Thais on how to solve their traffic jams. But even he finally threw up his hands and agreed it was hopeless.

Sure, we were warned about trying to cross the streets in Bangkok, but that didn't keep us from trying —especially if we learned that something was two bahts cheaper on the other side. (One baht is equal to five cents.)

When we were back on the plane, I looked around at all the guys and gals comparing purchases. Fran Jeffries was wearing a ring on every finger. Redd Foxx, sitting across the aisle, had a real ivory necklace around his neck and was snapping pictures of everyone with two of the many cameras he had bought.

Lola Falana bought thirty porcelain elephants weighing some ninety pounds each. She only paid about three bucks apiece for them, but it certainly would have been cheaper for her to ride them back to the states than to ship them back.

That shopping day for Operation Bob Hope must have been a shocker to the Thai people, who are extremely warm and polite. (What's more, the women there are more beautiful than those I have seen in any other country.) But even the nicest American Mrs. Jekyll turns into Mrs. Hyde when she's out hunting a bargain.

When I returned to the United States, and a saleslady in a department store said, "That will be $29.95, please," I found myself saying, "I'll give you $20.00 and not a penny more!"

Every one of us, including the very young, were exhausted each night when we returned to the Erewan Hotel, our home base in Bangkok, after visiting one or two military camps a day. We were all hot, dirty and bitten up by mosquitoes; the only one still filled with energy and pep was Robert Hope, who looked as fresh as he did when we started out at 7 A.M. that morning.

When we got back on the plane, after being out in the broiling sun for hours and hours, Bob would doze off for maybe fifteen minutes. He believes catnaps were what kept him going. On the plane, between bases, he would sit up front with his writers working away at the next monologue—he had a different one for every region.

And it always amazes me to hear people say, "Sure, Bob Hope goes out on these military trips. He does it to make money. After all, he gets paid back and plenty more from that TV special he does for NBC each year." Actually I'm told it costs Bob about $250,000 out of his own pocket to make each one of those Christmas trips.

# Dolores Hope Had 'Em Crying

After visiting so many military bases with Bob Hope in Asia, it's difficult to choose the most memorable moment of the entire trip—there were so many.

When we started out, I was told by people who had been with him before that there is usually one thing during a performance that grabs you more than any other.

Mine happened aboard the aircraft carrier *Midway* at sea a few miles outside of Singapore. I started out laughing, as I sat on the hard floor of the deck along with six thousand men (mostly sailors) to see the show for the first time in its entirety. It was fun to watch the reactions as the guys went wild as Miss World and all the other young beauty-contest winners made their first entrance on a shiny new stage. You see, another carrier had received its notice to move out, and as it passed the *Midway* it transmitted this message: "Can you use a brand-new stage?" Right out there in the Indian Ocean, the stage was transferred from the one ship to the other.

The men howled with glee at Bob Hope and Redd Foxx's monologues and again at the skit they did together. They whistled like crazy for Fran Jeffries' figure and for her singing. They acted like it was the first time they had ever seen a girl when Lola Falana sang and danced. They applauded Roman Gabriel, who joined up with us for this, the almost last leg of the journey.

But it was when Mrs. Bob Hope (Dolores) came out just before the finale that it all really got to me. Six thousand men and boys stood up (as gentlemen) without being prodded to do so, when she made her entrance, then sat down again and became very still while she sang "White Christmas."

I looked around at all those young faces, many of them with their heads lowered now, trying to hide their emotions, while hundreds of others sat there with tears streaming down their faces, as she finished with "And May All Your Christmases Be Home." I looked away from them, as they tried to do from their ship-mates, because the tears were streaming down my face, too.

Several times before that day at sea, I had a lump in my throat during performances. But until then I had not actually cried.

Dolores Hope asked the boys to sing "White Christmas" with her, which they did to a man. When she finished they again stood up for a quiet moment, then burst into wild applause. Mrs. Hope repre-sented "home" and "Mom" to those six thousand guys. This, for me, was the most touching moment of the entire trip. I'll never forget those young faces trying hard, but not successfully, to hold back the tears.

If "they" (whoever they are), who make the deci-sions to wage wars could experience that moment, maybe there would be no more wars. I'd sure like to think so.

# A "Thank You" Prayer

Barbara Stanwyck, who lives for today and tomorrow and only seldom for yesterday, did, however, sit up late one night talking with me about her childhood. And some of the things she said are now permanently etched in my memory.

"I cannot recall, Shirley," she said, "ever hearing anyone say to me as a child, 'I love you!'" Barbara spoke of having no memories of her father or mother, since both had died soon after she was born. "I tell you this," she continued, "only to make you aware of how fortunate you are to have been surrounded by so much love all of your life. Both your parents who love you are still alive. You have your husband, your two children and even members of your husband's family who adore you.

"But I'm grateful for what I do have. Every night before I go to sleep I thank God for what he has given me. When I awake each morning I again thank God for being here this day."

Barbara Stanwyck, that night, made me totally aware of how lucky I have been all of my life. Until she underlined everything, I now know I had been taking all those blessings for granted.

Aside from being loved by and in turn loving my immediate family, I now think of how fortunate I am to be working at something I look forward to doing each day.

I love meeting people, and certainly as a newspaper columnist I get to meet all kinds: actors, politicians, authors, prominent businessmen and women and even some fascinating underworld characters. Instead of being paid to do my job I ought to pay for the privilege of being able to work at and in it (a fact I hope my bosses, if they are reading this, won't take seriously).

Actually, it was author Irving Wallace who, when he heard I had an offer from Doubleday to write a book, insisted I sit down and start it at once—which I did that very night.

Several months ago in Philadelphia as I was waiting to go on a "Mike Douglas Show," I listened to his partially ad-lib introduction as he said, "And now gossip columnist Shirley Eder will come out and join us. No—I take that back! Shirley is not a gossip columnist. She is something more, so let's just call her Columnist Shirley Eder." I was thrilled to hear that introduction because I want to be recognized as a news columnist rather than one who just gossips.

I cannot find it in my heart to deliberately hurt someone for the sake of an item. Perhaps in my business that's not so advantageous but at least I sleep well at night.

Just after I was married, Edward said, "I'm all for your continuing with your career, Shirley, providing you don't go out of your way to be mean or rotten for the sake of success. If and when you become successful, the day you use your column as a personal weapon against someone you don't like, that's the day I am going to ask you to give it up."

Over the years there have been many times when I have been angry on a personal level with a prominent person and have sat down at the typewriter to get even. But as I go to type out whatever evil thing it is I have planned to say, Edward's words seem always to come back to me, and my fingers become atrophied and I just can't strike the keys.

Now, that may sound Pollyannaish, but there are so many ways to tell a story and so many stories to tell without having to be hurtful.

I don't pretend to like everybody. Nobody does! I don't like Raquel Welch, for instance, so I try to check out thoroughly the things I tell about her before putting them in print.

There are so many people I write about that I like and love. And there are times I must tell things about these people that perhaps they would rather not see in print. My friends—at least the real ones—understand that it's my job.

Sure, I have held back stories—up to a point. If someone is having marital difficulties and asks me not to print the fact because there is still a chance of patching things up, I'll keep their secret—until they have actually decided to make a definite break.

Sometimes when I do this I am scooped by other columnists which usually upsets me momentarily. But eight times out of ten I get the real story first. My job is to report the news, not to invent it or to write merely from hearsay.

How lucky I have been in life to have known so many wonderful people and to be able to call some of them "friends."

There is Mary Martin, whom I adore. And Julie Andrews, one of the truly delightful people in this world; columnist Bert Bacharach and his wife, Irma, and their son "Haps" (the famous composer Burt Bacharach). I am extremely fond of Joan Blondell, Anne Jeffreys and her husband, Bob Sterling, and Lena Horne.

By now, you know how much Kathryn Grayson means to me and my family.

When I was a kid doing those radio shows on station WINS in New York I got to know Al Jolson and Sophie Tucker. As the years went on I was fortunate to know Bert Lahr on both professional and social levels. I like all the Gabors—especially Zsa Zsa—who always make news for those of us in the column business. Gloria Swanson is a friend, as is Melina Mercouri and so are the Henry Fondas. I have spent time with Billy Graham and Mrs. Franklin Delano Roosevelt. I have been a guest at the White House and have interviewed Elvis Presley. I met the Beatles when they were together and have by choice avoided meeting the Rolling Stones. Ozzie and Harriet Nelson are very special people who beautifully brought up their famous sons, David and Rick Nelson. Sammy Davis, Jr., is my friend, as are the Marty Allens.

Columnists tend to look with disdain on the public relations men and women who feed them news, knowing that what they say cannot always be factual because of the reams of material they must continually send out about each client.

I do not look with disdain upon the majority of press agents. I realize that I need them as much as they need me. Sure, they are not all, like Caesar's wife, above reproach. It takes time to get to know whom you can really believe, and by now I pretty much know whom to trust.

Over a period of many years I have put my faith in and have not been disappointed by publicity men Lee Solters, Charles Pomerantz, John Strauss, Dick Guttman, Paul Wasserman, Bob Perilla and Mike Hall. When they tell me something, I believe them. There are many other good firms I work with such as Rogers, Cowan and Brenner, David Kramer, Betsy Nolan and many others.

From time to time I look back on some special moments. For instance: the opening-night party of *I Do! I Do!*, in Rockefeller Center's Rainbow Room. Mary Martin and her costar Robert Preston, who had just given wonderful performances, paid tribute to Gower

Champion for so brilliantly directing and choreographing their show. When the dance music started, Gower took his wife, Marge, into his arms and they danced together as they had done so many times in films and on the stage.

By then Marge had retired to be a wife to Gower and a mother to their two sons. That night in a room on top of New York City they were reunited as the beautiful dancing Champions. Everyone stood on the side lines watching and applauding; little did any one of us there ever think they would separate as man and wife. Yet, as of this writing, Marge has filed for divorce.

I will always remember Ginger Rogers, who said to me, although I was a stranger at the time, "You have honest eyes; tell me the truth about the show and my performance." Over a period of years since then I have been able to tell Ginger the truth about anything. Well, almost anything. The one thing I have learned not to discuss with her is the manner in which she wears her hair.

And it seems to me she has done all right with or without such advice from any one of us.

I could go on and on with special moments, but that is a whole other book.

Barbara Stanwyck, in your childhood no one may ever have said, "I love you." But now you are loved by millions of people you have never met and by those few of us fortunate enough to have been accepted in your life. I love you very much, Barbara, as does my husband, Edward, my son, John and my daughter Toni. I have learned valuable lessons from you and hope to continue learning from you for years to come.

I always said, "Thank you, God" when I went to sleep at night. But it was you who pointed out how much I really have to be thankful for. So now, I too say, "Thank you, God," again when I awake each morning.

## ABOUT THE AUTHOR

Shirley Eder began her career just out of high school by hosting a daily woman's radio show in New York. She was stage-struck then and still is—even after writing a daily syndicated column for major newspapers all over the country. Her phone bills bring joy to the hearts of AT&T stockholders—but strike terror in the heart of her husband, Edward.